ARGUMENT

ALAN HARRIS & GERALD GURNEY

Contents

Cambridge University Press

Cambridge
London · New York · Melbourne

Acknowledgements

We wish to thank the many people who have given us permission to reproduce their letters in this book and we appreciate the help we have received from newspapers and periodicals in finding some of the correspondents. We have tried to trace everyone whose letters we have used and we can only offer our apologies if we have offended anyone whom we have unwittingly failed to consult.

Our thanks are also due to *The Times*, *The Daily Telegraph* (and Peter Simple), *The Guardian* (and Gillian Tindall, Mary Stott, Margaret Lickards, John Grigg and Valentine Perera), *Daily Express*, *The Observer*, *Sunday Mirror*, *East Anglian Daily Times*, *Essex County Standard*, *Colchester Express*, *Kent Messenger* and *New Statesman* (and Kathleen Gibberd, Mervyn Jones and Magnus Turnstile) for permission to reproduce articles, to Ruth Harrison for permission to reproduce an extract from her book, *Animal Machines*, which appeared in *The Observer*, to Her Majesty's Stationery Office for permission to reproduce extracts from the Newsom Report and the Licensing Act and to Richard Findlater and the Society of Authors for permission to reproduce an extract from *The Book Writers*.

We are also grateful to Jack Cross for helping us to formulate the idea for this book, and to the Commerce Department of the Sir Anthony Deane School for secretarial assistance, and to Sergeant Firmin of the Harwich Police Force for help well outside the ordinary course of duty.

Published by the Syndics of the Cambridge University Press
The Pitt Building, Trumpington Street, Cambridge CB2 1RP
Bentley House, 200 Euston Road, London NW1 2DB
32 East 57th Street, New York, NY 10022, USA
296 Beaconsfield Parade, Middle Park, Melbourne 3206, Australia

Library of Congress catalogue card number: 67-29751

ISBN 0 521 05216 5

First published 1968
Reprinted 1969, 1970, 1976, 1977

Printed in Great Britain by
Lowe & Brydone Printers Limited, Thetford, Norfolk

Introduction

All teachers of English know that newspapers can supply excellent material for use in class. Such material can, for example, be the starting point for discussion of current affairs, for the analysis of various styles of writing, or as the basis of impromptu exercises in comprehension or précis. The advantages of using newspapers lie in their topicality and variety, and in the fact that newspapers are read in most homes, whereas books are not. The disadvantages are practical ones: it is difficult to supply all members of a class with copies of the same newspaper, and it is very time-consuming for the teacher to comb through several papers in search of worth-while subjects, especially of the sort contained in this book. We have, for example, been able to include articles from a newspaper together with a complete sequence of letters which followed in subsequent editions.

All of the material could be used in many ways, most obviously, perhaps, as the starting point for discussions on a wide range of topics of general interest. However, we have particularly tried to select articles and letters whose main interest lies in:

a) the conceptual thinking involved,

b) the *manner* of expression and *technique* of persuasion,

c) the *quality* of reasoning and argument.

For example, where material about the school-leaving age is presented, we envisage that pupils will examine the effectiveness and fairness of the various arguments rather than use the material as a starting point for the airing of their own views, although in this instance there may be a high degree of personal involvement. Of course, the teacher may wish pupils to pursue both courses, but it is with the former in mind that we have planned the book.

In other words, this is really a book intended to facilitate the informal study of logic.

Most books on Logic, or 'Clear Thinking', seem to us to be faulty in one or more of the following ways:

a) some, concerned with formal logic, use dreary, out-dated and artificial examples;

b) some, concerned with labelling 101 faults in everyday argument, grossly oversimplify the position, so that the pupil will recognise the 101 and fail to appreciate the infinite subtlety of real argument;

c) most are rather destructive, and do little to encourage a positive appreciation of clear logical thinking (some of our extracts are specifically chosen for this purpose);

d) most are suitable for only a very limited range of readers.

By using newspaper extracts on a wide variety of interesting topics, we have tried to avoid the first of these faults. The others are avoided simply by leaving it to the teacher to decide how much, and to what depth, he wants to teach. Thus, the book can be used in all types of secondary schools, as well as in Colleges of Further Education, W.E.A. classes, and so on.

All the extracts in this book have been used successfully by the authors in both grammar and secondary modern schools with pupils of 14 or over. Our approach is usually as follows:

First, the material is read aloud by a pupil (the teacher might undesirably by his tone or manner imply a particular interpretation of the content). If necessary, the teacher then sparks off analysis by putting a few open-ended questions of the sort contained at the end of this book. It will be noticed that none of these questions is of the 'comprehension' sort, that none implies any personal judgment on the part of the questioner, and that in one way or another they are all aimed at directing attention to the writer's thought processes, concepts, and methods of argument. None of them merely asks for the pupil's opinion on the subject in question.

The approach we have found successful can easily be gathered from these suggested questions, but many teachers will doubtless prefer to ignore these questions and handle the material in their own way. We have kept the questions separate from the text since if the pupils can *see*, without effort, the sort of question they should frame for themselves, then they will not themselves develop the habit of doing the real work.

We have found that with practice many pupils are capable of conducting an entire lesson for themselves, with no help at all from the teacher; but with less able pupils it will still be necessary for the teacher to ask some questions to prevent the discussion from becoming side-tracked into a mere exchange of personal opinions.

With regard to the extracts which follow, we have chosen subjects which we have found to be of interest to modern teenagers (and we have tried not to underestimate them) and which provoke interesting conceptual analysis. The printers have preserved something of the original appearance of the extracts since very often the newspaper's presentation of the article (headlines, type, etc.) condition the reader's response. All passages are complete as published except where indicated.

One complaint we have already received is that too much of the material comes from the 'quality press' and far too little from the papers usually found in many pupils' homes. In the first place we had indeed hoped for a better balance, but months of combing through the popular press has produced only a depressingly small number of items where the quality of thought is interesting even for its badness. For the most part the readers' letters are anecdotal, like the following which appeared in the *Daily Mirror:*

Grrrrr!

This letter comes from Abergavenny, Monmouthshire:

On the envelope of a letter I received was the Post Office frank: 'The Country Code. Keep your dog under control.'

Right underneath was my name, which happens to be . . .

Mr. D. Woof.

They were barking up the right tree!

This sort of correspondence is fascinating, though not altogether suitable for the limited purposes of this book. We would certainly be grateful, however, to any readers of this book who could refer us, for the sake of future editions, to suitable material in the popular press.

A. H. & G.N.G.

School till 16

Introduction (*from the Newsom Report*)

There is very little doubt that among our children there are reserves of ability which can be tapped, if the country wills the means. One of the means is a longer school life. There is, surely, something of an anomaly in the fact that whereas a five-year secondary course is regarded as an essential minimum for our ablest children in the grammar schools and for those of very limited capacities indeed, in schools for the educationally sub-normal, less is demanded for the large majority of children who neither progress as quickly as the first group nor are as severely limited in their potential as the second.

Our terms of reference imply, and the whole argument of our report assumes, a school-leaving age of 16 for everyone. We have again considered the position with great care, and we have unhesitatingly come to the same conclusion as the Council reached in 1959: 'This is a duty which society owes all its young citizens'. The evidence presented to us makes it clear that in the last few years there has been a marked strengthening of conviction in this matter, both among those professionally concerned with education and among the interested general public. The percentage of pupils who voluntarily remain at school beyond the minimum age of 15 has doubled in the secondary modern schools since 1958,* and this in itself testifies to an increasing confidence in the schools and to a belief on the part of many parents in the value of a longer education for their children. Already in some modern schools, pupils are voluntarily remaining not only for a fifth but for a sixth year, and we have little doubt when the formal school-leaving age is raised to 16, there will be more pupils voluntarily choosing to stay to 17 and even 18.

But the decision to raise the school-leaving age should not therefore continue to be deferred and progress left to follow its voluntary course. There are still too many boys and girls who, otherwise, will leave at the earliest possible moment, whatever their potential abilities, because outside pressures are too much for them. Again and again teachers confirm that the pupils with whom we are especially concerned stand to gain a great deal in terms of personal development as well as in the consolidating of attainments from a longer period of full-time education—but it is just

---

* In 1962, rather more than one-sixth of the age group in secondary modern schools for the country as a whole, and a very much higher percentage for some individual schools and areas.

these boys and girls who most readily succumb to the attractions of the pay-packet and the bright lights it commands.

21. Besides, in the national interest we cannot afford to go on waiting. Others are already ahead of us. It is true that we start school a year earlier than most countries, but there is no reason to assume that the majority of our children are ahead of other people's at the age of 15 when they leave school. In the United States nearly two-thirds of the population are at High Schools until the age of 18, and there is currently much concern over 'the drop-outs', many of whom have stayed at school until 16. France, with problems of shortages of teachers and of accommodation comparable with our own, has already raised the school-leaving age from 14 to 16 for all the pupils who started school in or after 1959.

Recommendation

An immediate announcement should be made that the school-leaving age will be raised to 16 for all pupils entering the secondary schools from 1965 onwards. The year in which the new leaving age first becomes operative would then be 1969-70, when the number of 15-year-olds involved is relatively low.

From 'Half Our Future', a report of the central Advisory Council for Education (England) 1963.

(A) SCHOOL TILL 16

IF the Government has any doubts as to the wisdom or necessity of raising the school leaving age to 16, it has suppressed them. The decision will not take effect till the educational year 1970-1. This will not be soon enough to satisfy the Newsom Committee or the National Union of Teachers. Both of these bodies wanted the leaving age raised in 1969, a year in which, according to Newsom, there would be relatively few 15-year-olds in the schools. Disagreeing, Sir EDWARD BOYLE yesterday expressed grounds for even more caution than he has shown. The dip in school numbers which was expected in the late 1960s will not now, so he tells us, materialise at all. There is accordingly no time at which the leaving age could be raised " without the risk that staffing standards would be seriously worsened." By his own expressed logic, we have either to postpone the decision " almost indefinitely" or else to go on tolerating staffing standards which " will not be what we would like ideally to see."

It is a question of priorities. This accepted, who would put raising the leaving age at the top?

Even the NUT, which has a natural vested interest in the infinite expansion of education, emphasised that the leaving age should not be raised at the expense of other commitments. Already there are many 14-year-olds—a third of them, some teachers say—who derive no obvious pleasure or profit from remaining at school. These children jeopardise the education of those who would benefit by it.

Even in 1970, according to Sir EDWARD, we shall be short of some 35,000 teachers. For some reason he hopes that the decision to raise the leaving age will of itself lure more people, especially graduates, into teaching. Of course, there are among teachers dedicated exceptions to whom the more invincible their pupils' ignorance, the greater the challenge, the greater the joy at each infinitesimal advance. Yet these are exceptions. They must be set against the numberless hearts, graduate and others, which have been broken by the task of instructing the uninstructible—a task soon to be further prolonged. How would Sir EDWARD himself like it? The limits of what is politically possible seem sometimes to exclude all good sense. What otherwise would be wrong with leaving matters alone, with this proviso: that no one should leave school before 16 unless parents, teachers and the pupil were all agreed that this was best?

Editorial 'The Daily Telegraph' 28 January 1964

(B) SIR—Thank you for your excellently reasoned leader " School till 16." Let us hope that it will induce the Minister to think again. He must realise that, apart from a relatively small number of political and educational theorists and axe-grinders, few in the country will view the new measure with enthusiasm and many parents will deeply resent it.

Much bitterness has already been caused by the Minister's edict that 15-year-olds may not leave school at Easter but must await the end of the summer term.

Seen against the general background of education and a deficiency of 35,000 teachers, the proposed measure would have a disastrous effect on the whole pattern of education. For to drag back to school these reluctant and sometimes mutinous pupils would further stretch the under-strength teaching force and necessitate larger classes (and therefore less individual progress) throughout the educational system.

In your sanity you ask a question: " Why change a system which works efficiently?" The public will re-echo your " Why?"

Yours faithfully,
G. G. MURPHY,
Head Master.

London, S.E.16

(C) Sir—I must object to the description " uninstructible " applied to boys in school in your leader. How easy it is to condemn other people's children in this way.

I have been teaching in a secondary modern school for many years and am convinced that, in the vast majority of cases, *we* have failed when a boy dislikes school or fails to learn.

Does a hospital keep only patients who are well and throw out those seriously ill? Why then should we reject quickest those boys who need most our care and attention?

You write that some teachers say that a third of the 14-year-olds derive no obvious pleasure or profit from remaining at school. This remark applies equally well to the teachers who make it.

I welcome the change. Now on to 17! Yours faithfully,
V. L. COOMBES.
Bovey Tracey, Devon.

(D) Sir—For the extra year at school not only more teachers are needed but, judging by present results, a better system of teaching.

As an employer of labour in a large business I find the contem-

5

porary teenager almost illiterate. Some of them can barely read or write; all of them are completely ignorant of the most elementary knowledge, *e.g.* the filing clerk who, hearing someone mention Christopher Columbus, asked: "Who was Columbus?" A minute's explanation from me, plus a well-known rhyming mnemonic, fixed the facts in her mind, and later I heard her instructing another ignoramus.

We employers accept the raw material and do the work which the teachers seem to have overlooked. By all means let the children stay at school for another year if they show promise; otherwise hand them over to us and we can at least teach them to be useful.   Yours faithfully,
                    C. N. WRIGHT.
London, N.W.11.

'The Daily Telegraph'
31 January 1964

THE "UNINSTRUCTIBLE"
Ⓖ School Discipline's Young Destroyers

SIR—It was interesting to me as a retired teacher of 40 years' service to read the letters concerning the proposed raising of the school-leaving age to 16 for all pupils irrespective of circumstances.

One letter in particular, by Mr. V. L. Coombes, of Bovey Tracey (Jan. 31), was so full of confidence that he applauded the day when it would be raised even to the age of 17. His remarks, however, concerning those who dared suggest that certain boys were un-instructible are hardly likely to be appreciated by thousands of teachers in big city areas who have had experience of difficult 14/15-year-olds who refuse even to match up to a reasonable standard of behaviour, and who, though in the minority, destroy the discipline of the whole form, and I even suggest school.

It is the teachers, Mr. Coombes says, that have failed. Oh to be able to transfer this gentleman, in his comfortable school in Bovey Tracey, to several I have seen and experienced, where students have been forced to withdraw from the classroom almost in tears, and where experienced teachers have been obliged to call others into the room for support.

Little is known of these facts, since it is hardly possible for heads to admit that there is trouble in their particular schools. Heads are not to blame in these cases; it is the district into which they have been allocated, plus the continuous interference of authorities into the manner in which they would deal with lads who are bullies and "uninstructible."

How different from the quiet country schools it is to be in charge of a form of 35 boys (14-year-olds) in a secondary modern where at least nine of them are on "probation" for the first or even second time and where their parents are behind the bad boys and not in support of the teachers. I regret to say that only when one

has left the schools for good is one able to bring to light these facts, and these will be denied by many eager to toe the official line.
            Yours faithfully,
Hastings.   R. TORBETT.

Ⓗ
SIR—What effect will raising the school-leaving age again have except to increase the already astronomical cost of education?

Knowledge cannot be pumped in like air in a tyre, and the attempt to do this *en masse* is a frequent cause of failure.

It is an indisputable fact that some children can and some cannot benefit ∥∥∥∥∥∥∥∥∥∥∥∥∥∥∥∥∥ from further formal instruction, and very often the education of the latter starts when they enter industry, simply ∥∥∥∥∥∥∥∥∥∥∥∥∥∥∥∥∥ because they gain confidence and see the results of their efforts put to practical use, and of course receive some payment for the effort.

LETTERS TO THE EDITOR

I suggest that with proper safeguards many children would be better off working.

On the other hand children who want to and are capable of deriving benefit can choose to stay at school. This would certainly help to prevent the restlessness and sense of frustration so often found in fifth and sixth forms.

Many teachers privately agree, but so-called educationalists tend to look at the problem only from the standpoint of their own intelligence, which is often lop-sided, and so fail to see the wood because of the trees.

During the past 30 years or so education has advanced rapidly; so has juvenile delinquency. Is it pure coincidence?
            GEO. A. MUIRHEAD.
London, S.W.16.

'The Daily Telegraph'
5 February 1964

Ⓔ
From
    Miss J. M. QUENNELL, M.P.

SIR—Your correspondents have attacked the Government's decision to raise the school-leaving age in the year 1970-1 solely on the grounds of present, 1964, standards of expediency.

No one could fault their arguments if the Government's decision had applied to the coming educational year. But obviously in the intervening years there must be changes—not least in our attitude towards the purpose of the five-year course.

The weakness of the present four-year course is that it is not long enough to provide a genuinely secondary education. The first year all too often has been diagnostic, the second and sometimes third remedial, and the remaining year overshadowed by the prospect of leaving.

The weakness of our attitude towards secondary education is that we do not recognise the essential connection with life and work. The Newsom Report emphasised the need to focus the child's mind upon its subsequent post-school career and the importance of relating its educational course to its choice of prospective employment.

Fail in this, and the course will be remote, unreal, vague and meaningless to the pupil. Then indeed you will have a school of mutineers —and rightly!

To succeed, we must greatly strengthen the machinery of transition between school and work. The youth employment service must come into the schools *before* the pupil's last school year *begins*.

In consultation with the careers staff, the pupil and the parents, his choice of job must be decided sufficiently in advance of leaving school for his last year to be practically related to the future, which he must be able to see for himself.
            Yours faithfully,
            J. M. QUENNELL.
House of Commons.

Ⓕ
Sir—By all means raise the school-leaving age, but let the last six months be devoted to the meaning of being a good citizen and the responsibilities of parenthood.

So many of the young people to-day are sadly lacking in the meaning of these two very important aspects of life, and many parents are obviously unable to set an example or impart the knowledge.   Yours faithfully,
            FRANCES SHELDON.
London, N.W.6.

'The Daily Telegraph'
8 February 1964

(I) Sir—In his interesting letter debating the value of raising the school-leaving age Mr. G. A. Muirhead (Feb. 5) fails to appreciate the problems of choosing " those children who want to and are capable of deriving benefit " from staying on at school for an extra year. Apart from the grammar school " streams " whose problems of selection are a study in themselves, does he suggest that all those who want to will benefit and all those who do not want to will not benefit from a further year?

Who helps a child of 15 make up his mind? The parents who might be quite content to have an additional wage to help balance the family budget? The teacher, faced with ever increasing sizes of classes? Or is the attraction of pseudo-independence brought by one's first pay packet to be allowed to decide this important step? It could be argued that such a step is in no one's interest.

It is surely possible for a curriculum to be created to do for the 15-year-old what the sixth year *should* do at a higher level. Namely, not instruct the set school subjects for a longer period, maintaining the rigid teacher-pupil relationship, but instil in a more informal atmosphere those qualities of responsibility and citizenship which Mr. Muirhead claims to be lacking in modern youth, and so prepare the new citizens to shoulder their future responsibilities and resist the excessive influences of sections of our affuent society. Yours faithfully,
KENNETH W. RUDDIMAN,
Cumberland.

'The Daily Telegraph'
7 February 1964

Crisis (J)

" LOOK out, boys! Here comes the press gang! " At the look-out's urgent words, the saloon bar was a scene of frenzied activity as drinkers hurriedly downed their drinks and vanished into secret hiding-places in the walls, under the counter or up the chimney. As the grim-faced Ministry of Education posse tramped in, the bar was deserted and the landlord's face was a mask of innocence.

" Right, men! " roared the leader, " take the place apart! I know there are scrimshankers here! By God, we'll take every man Jack of them and make teachers of them yet!"

By 1980, with the school leaving age raised to 18 and the shortage of teachers acute, such scenes were a daily commonplace throughout the country. The teachers' training colleges were full of sullen pressed men being licked into shape by instructors who made the old-fashioned sergeant-major seem like a kindergarten raffia-work demonstrator.

Yet the Ministry of Education was still far short of the target of four million teachers, which must be reached, Progressives pointed out, if the country were not to sink without trace. There was a call for severe penalties, including flogging, for those who harboured deserters.

There was also an ingenious suggested scheme by which the enormous louts of 17 and 18 who now terrorised the secondary modern schools would themselves become teachers on alternate days. After all, in a democratic country, it was not the quality of education which counted, but the quantity.

'Peter Simple'
'The Daily Telegraph'
31 January 1964

Drinking Laws

Introduction

LICENSING ACT 1964
PART III   PERMITTED HOURS

Prohibition of sale, etc., of intoxicating liquor outside permitted hours.

60. i) Subject to the following provisions of this Part of the Act, the permitted hours in licensed premises shall be:

a) on weekdays, other than Christmas Day or Good Friday, the hours from eleven in the morning to half-past ten in the evening, with a break of two and a half hours beginning at three in the afternoon; and

b) on Sundays, Christmas Day and Good Friday, the hours from twelve noon to half-past ten in the evening, with a break of five hours beginning at two in the afternoon.

(A) *ARCHAIC LAW*

Sir—It is my opinion that the British drinking laws are archaic, that the laws should be abolished and, therefore, that we should be able to purchase alcoholic drinks at any time during the day and night.

Has any reader any views on the subject, or any reasons for wanting to retain the law as it stands?   Yours faithfully,
M. S. GARFIELD.
Middlesex

'The Daily Telegraph'
2 September 1963

Drinking Laws Are a Laughing-Stock

Promoting Drunkenness

(B) Sir—Mr. M. S. Garfield is right. Anyone who has lived in a Continental country for any length of time knows that our drinking laws are the laughing-stock of modern countries.

There is no doubt they have promoted the very thing they were meant to prevent—drunkenness. During my 15 years on the Continent I could go into a café (or sit in the sun if I wished) for a beer. My wife could have her glass of wine or a coffee, my daughter her ice-cream. We took our refreshment as a family unit, and the café was not enveloped in a sinister atmosphere unsuitable for children where it was sinful to have a drink between the hours of 3 p.m. and 6 p.m.

Like many of our laws, those governing drink are not based on common sense but on the intolerance of a minority. Belgium consumes much more beer per head of the population than does Britain, but it is far harder to find a drunk there than here.

Yours faithfully,
H. C. WILSON.
Devon

(C) Sir—I have just returned from a holiday on the Continent, and it was refreshing to be able to take a drink when I wanted one without first having to look at my watch to make sure that "they were open." It was equally refreshing to be served with a drink at 10.30 p.m. instead of being ushered out of the bar by the words "Time, gentlemen, please."

It would be nonsense to say that we could not alter our drinking laws. The system of opening all day (and half the night) works perfectly well on the Continent. Why not here? Yours faithfully,
P. W. D. TANSLEY.
London, E.7.

(D) Sir—Mr. M. S. Garfield's letter prompts me to suggest that licensees should be permitted to serve liquor 24 hours a day, with a compulsory minimum of six hours a day, on condition that the particular hours chosen by them remain unchanged for 12 months and be posted so as to be readable outside their premises.
Yours faithfully,
L. M. LILLEY.
London, S.W.1

(E) Sir—One has only to read of the increased road accidents since the extra licensing laws were granted to realise we want less facilities for buying alchohol rather than more. Yours faithfully,
London, N.10.   N. SHUTES.

'The Daily Telegraph'
4 September 1963

Minority Language

CYMRAEG   VOLUME   TONE

Compulsory Welsh

(A) Sir,—In these days of shifting populations and the re-siting of industries, do non-Welsh parents realise that if their work happens to take them to Wales, their children will find themselves compulsorily taught Welsh, with no parental right of withdrawal in most areas? It may be educationally desirable to teach children something of the history and culture of the community in which they live, and polite to teach them how to pronounce local place-names correctly, but these ends can be better served than by wasting several hours a week of valuable school time in acquiring a smattering of a minority language.

Purley.   Jean Cardy

'The Observer'
19 June 1966

THE RIGHT TO CHOOSE

(B) SIR,—Mrs Jean Cardy objects to the teaching of Welsh to the children of non-Welsh parents whose work takes them to Wales. I wonder if she would object to the teaching of French, German or Icelandic to the children of people who go to live in those countries, or to the teaching of English to the children of Pakistanis who come here?

Anyone who adopts a foreign country as his home is under an obligation to respect the language and traditions of that country — common sense would demand this even if courtesy did not. And such respect is not possible without learning the language. Mrs Cardy evidently subscribes to the fallacy that Welsh is a kind of beastly peasant jargon, of no practical or aesthetic worth, perpetuated solely in order to annoy the English and to enable two price ranges to be charged in the shops.

Preston.   Alan Howard

★

(C) Sir,—I was very pleased to read Mrs Cardy's letter last Sunday.

When I came to live in Glamorgan, where my husband now works, I was concerned to find that my children would have to spend a *minimum* of 15 per cent of their most formative educational years at junior school in studying the Welsh language.

In this county only about one person in four has a command of Welsh, and fewer still—sentiment aside—can claim it as their first everyday means of communication. The members of the education committee are primarily elected to office on a party ticket, and their knowledge of and views on educational matters —if any—are irrelevant at the polls. It is doubtful if their election can be construed as a mandate to impose their views on all and sundry. Vociferous lobbying by the teaching profession in favour of Welsh has a solid foundation of self-interest.

Further, this arrogant and unjustifiable discounting of the views of many parents directly conflicts with one of the guiding principles of the 1944 Education Act, where Section 76 specifically lays down the right of all parents to choose within reason how their children are educated.

(Mrs) Elizabeth S. MacBean
Bridgend.

'The Observer'
26 June 1966

9

Dressing up for the Wedding

MARY STOTT talking about weddings

AS SEEMED proper and honest for an agnostic family, my brothers and I were all married in register offices, quietly. All our children, churchgoers, backsliders, and agnostics alike, have been married in church, in full fig, with mobs of friends and relations invited to an hotel reception. Why? It puzzles and vexes me that these serious-minded young men, these clear-eyed, independent young women, should choose to make their marriage vows in ludicrously inappropriate clothes, surrounded by a costly, pretentious public charade.

My prejudices about weddings reveal me, I am afraid, as a feminist, a prude, and a petite bourgeoise. Wearing a long white gown doesn't make today's brides feel like sacrificial victims as they are led to the altar and handed over by Papa to the care of the bridegroom. I shouldn't think it would occur to any bride now to hand over half the price of the marriage licence, even with a giggle. They are sure of their equal status, and white is "dreamy," not symbolic.

As sexual intercourse, within or outside marriage, is so often and so easily talked about, today's brides aren't likely to be embarrassed at having all the world gaping at them on their way to the marriage bed. Though I do wonder how they can bear the insensitive ribaldry of confetti stuffed down their necks and into their suitcases, the boorishness of tin cans and lavatory paper tied on to their cars.

It must be the petite bourgeoise in me that resents the top hats. Toppers are for Top People, for Ascot, for royal garden parties. They are not for the likes of us. They make our menfolk, unused to wearing any kind of hat, let alone the exceedingly silly, uncomfortable, and old-fashioned topper, look foolish. (So, of course, they all sheepishly carry them, and two or three toppers usually have to be recovered from pews and hotel cloakrooms.) I don't like our men having to hire fancy dress to gratify the unadmitted snobbery of the bride.

Sound instinct

I do think that the instinct which makes people choose a church wedding is usually sound, even if to people like me it sometimes has a look of superstition, or vainglory. It takes a fair degree of moral earnestness to make the marriage promises with the same solemn sincerity in a register office as in a church. But whether the marriage is solemnised as a sacrament or is a simple statement of intention in front of a registrar is nothing to do with what I'm talking about—the absurdity of the dressing up and the extravagance of the festivities.

Extravagance—particularly the demands on the bride's parents. Alas, I think the real difference between us and our children is affluence. Our register office weddings were a matter of conviction; the simple family gatherings that followed were a matter of our attitude to money. It never occurred to us that our parents should fork out large sums of money to see us off in style. What money they could spare we gratefully accepted to help with equipping our homes. But at least two of our brides, when offered the choice between a largish cheque and a largish "do," insisted on the "do." (And in fact, of course, also did quite well for parental gifts.) Our attitude towards money was that you had to watch it or it would run away. Theirs is that affluence is natural and perpetual. So why not, if you want to, spend hundreds of pounds on a day's festivity? There's always more where that came from. It isn't fair to call the young greedy—most of them would cheerfully do it themselves if they just happened to have the hundreds in the bank and their parents hadn't.

But why do they want to spend money this way? Why not on a slap-up housewarming? Why, in this sceptical, iconoclastic age, when all the sacred cows are mocked at, when bridegrooms dote on "Private Eye" and brides crowd into the studio to watch programmes like BBC 3, does no one send up the mock society wedding? And has there ever been a bride who wrote little notes all round saying: "Would you please send a gift to Oxfam, not to me?"

'The Guardian'
9 May 1966

B

As a " clear-eyed and independent young woman " recently married to a " serious-minded young man," I was irritated to read Mary Stott's article on weddings (May 9).

I fail to see why Mrs Stott regards a long white gown as ' ludicrously inappropriate " for a church wedding, if she considers dressing-up permissible for Ascot and royal garden parties. If one considers marriage important, as obviously Mrs Stott does, then surely one must treat it is an occasion of some seriousness and not dress as if for a shopping expedition or afternoon tea.

The fact that I married in church and in white, though not being particularly religious, was due neither to snobbery nor the desire to appear as a pure and untouched maiden ; it was simply to stress the importance of this happening which deserved suitable recognition. And since today there is no decent alternative to a religious ceremony, I was not prepared to suffer the clinical supermarket atmosphere of the register office.

Admittedly the money spent on our reception (which my husband and I paid for) would have bought us our much needed carpet. But then we can buy carpets for the rest of our life.

Marriage *is* a festive occasion—a time for merrymaking and renewing of old friendships. I dare say we shall never have the chance to be so " extravagant " again, but then our marriage is a once-in-a-lifetime event.—Yours faithfully,

Georgina Mallalieu.

Hazel Grove, Cheshire.

Dressing up for the wedding

READERS' LETTERS

'The Guardian'
19 May 1966

C

OWING to our agnostic convictions, my husband and I were married in a register office. The reactions of friends and relatives, however, show why many people avoid this ceremony. My friends either pitied me because they assumed that my husband had previously been divorced, or were shocked, thinking that I was pregnant and a quiet and instant wedding was necessary. On all sides we were regarded with suspicion, pity, and even hostility.

Nor is this the only reason why people avoid such a ceremony. The register offices themselves are frequently in dismal parts of a town near juvenile courts, divorce courts, and undertakers. They are sometimes inadequately equipped. We had no waiting room before the ceremony, but were herded into a draughty, overcrowded corridor. There were no seats, even for elderly relatives. The actual room of the ceremony was superior to many of its kind, having a vase of flowers which provided the only colour in an otherwise brown room.

Many people with no Christian convictions would marry in a register office if it were not so obviously, at present, a poor second best. When it is recognised by public opinion as a true alternative to a church wedding, then less people will choose to be " surrounded by a pretentious public charade."—Yours faithfully,

(Mrs) **Susan M. Barker.**

Barnsley, Yorkshire

D

SURELY THE INSTINCT to arrange a wedding feast and to " dress up " for the marriage of two young people is a natural and good one ? What more fit occasion is there in the lives of most of us for a joyful celebration with friends and family than at the start of a new marriage ?

I share Mary Stott's dislike of " toppers." They seem to me to be increasingly inappropriate in our less class-conscious society. But white, as the symbol of chastity (love and respect for your husband or wife which includes but is not identified with pre-marital virginity), seems to me still most appropriate. I think many clergy try to show that it has a real meaning to those bridal couples who come to them.

As for the cheque to Oxfam, did not Christ say : " You have the poor with you always ? " Does charity, admittedly the greatest virtue, rule out festivity ? I hope not.—Yours faithfully,

Derek A. Smith

Macclesfield, Cheshire.

E

THE CHARADE of a church wedding is indeed all the things Mary Stott says it is : costly, pretentious and, most of all, irrelevant. But can it not also be seen as an effective safeguard against marrying someone in a fit of absence of mind ? All that bann reading, all the invitations, the publicity, the ritual, before finally standing up in front of all those friends and relations with the chosen man (looking, no doubt, like an embarrassed penguin) at one's side.

If you can go through all *that*, I am tempted to suggest that you are at least rather more likely to have thought twice about marrying, which is what, it appears, many separated or divorced couples once failed to do.

How effective a psychological safeguard this in fact is, could only be determined by a statistical survey, using register office marriages as the control group. I, for one, should be interested in the results.—Yours sincerely,

(Miss) **Anne Merrill.**

London SW 7.

F

WE TOLD OUR CHILDREN when they were quite young that we do not believe in church weddings (not unnaturally since we do not go to church or profess to be Christians), and that if they wanted such weddings they would have to save their own money to provide them ; we, as eternally hard-up parents, would not be prepared to pinch and save or get into debt for something we do not believe in.

I sometimes wonder whether these glamorous weddings are not partly responsible for the early marriages so many girls make today. To some very young people the idea of being the centre of attention, of looking " glam " or " dreamy " and of having shows of presents (this seems to me a particularly nauseating idea with its competitive implications) offers such dreams of glory she can hardly wait for the day. The whole business of very early marriages has become a fashion, and the girl who, quite sensibly, would prefer to wait until she is 24 or 25 may feel that the best men of her generation will have been mated by the time she reaches that age.

I wonder whether girls would be so keen on glamorous weddings if they had to save their own money to pay for them. The alternative of cheque or wedding makes it easier.

The white wedding business is, I believe, on the same level as the funeral business in America, a commercial racket.—Yours sincerely,

Mona Davidson.

West Linton, Peeblesshire.

G

AS A BLUSHING teenage bridesmaid in turquoise tulle at a " mock society wedding," I resolved that if I ever were to get married I should never cast myself for the rôle of leading lady/buffoon in an extravagant pantomime on the altar steps, or risk being a target for ribaldry and lavatory rolls at a reception. In fact, we married in a registrar's office with two witnesses, and if it was not exactly an awe-inspiring occasion it was at least painless, and had the additional virtues of being neither blasphemous nor expensive !

However, almost all my agnostic friends married recently have opted for a " do," and persist in regarding our non-wedding as wilfully abnormal, and probably as a prime example of killjoy meanness. Those who can be persuaded to see reason justify their own weddings as being primarily " for mother's sake." mother having usually struggled to give them an education and all the good things—including the fancy white dress—that she herself missed through poverty. Selfish I may be in having deprived my mother of a bit of vicarious glory, but I fail to see why, if they have really sacrificed principles and taste to please the family when marrying, they later draw the line at having their children christened !—Yours faithfully,

M.C.

Hertfordshire

11

Factory Farming

Ⓐ Life in the factory farm revolves entirely round profits, and animals are assessed purely for their ability to convert food into flesh, or "saleable products."

For the factory farmer and the agri-industrial world behind him, cruelty is acknowledged only where profitability ceases. If an animal continues to grow and put on flesh, he contends that his treatment of it cannot be said to be cruel, though it be crated up in the dark all its life.

To keep animals alive in the conditions in which they are reared, antibiotics are incorporated in their feed and heavier doses of drugs given at the least sign of flagging; growth stimulants, hormones and tranquillisers all have their part to play in the forcing of rapid conversion of animal feeding-stuffs into flesh.

Using these methods, factory farming has undoubtedly paid off. Each year sees the introduction of new niceties and the exploitation of ever more animals.

The poultry industry is a major example.

The day-old chicks are installed, 8,000 or 10,000 at a time, sometimes more, in long, windowless houses punctuated only with extractor fans in rows along the ridge of the roofs and air intake vents along the side walls. Inside a house the impression is of a long, wide, dark tunnel disappearing into the gloom, the floor covered with chickens as far as the eye can see. There are lights down each side, hoppers for food hang from the beams, and pipes keep a constant supply of water. The houses are sprayed regularly with insecticides to keep the chickens free of pests.

For the first two weeks the chicks are kept under warm brooders at a steady temperature of 90 deg. (that of a mother hen) in a constant, round-the-clock, bright light. Thus they are encouraged to eat and grow quickly. After two weeks the lights are changed to amber and go on and off for two hours round the clock. So the birds eat and sleep, eat and sleep, eat and sleep.

At six weeks they are big enough to feel the intensity of crowding, and too much light would mean too much fighting, so the lights are changed to 25 watt red—virtual darkness—and these go on and off round the clock every two hours. So they exist for the last four weeks of their short lives almost immobile, their only function to put on weight.

Many broilermen have their chickens de-beaked to avoid feather pecking and fighting in the later stages. According to *The Smallholder* (January 6, 1962), "feather-pecking and cannibalism has increased to a formidable extent in late years, due, no doubt, to the changes in technique and the swing towards completely intensive management of laying flocks and table poultry. Feather-pecking . . . is often the forerunner of cannibalism and for that reason it should be regarded as a dangerous vice."

Conditions are so crowded that any disease can sweep through the house very rapidly. "I am allowed an extra 2 per cent day-old chicks from the hatchery," one broilerman told me

" to allow for mortality." We noticed the pile of dead birds by the door. " They suffer mostly from respiratory diseases and cancer," he added, " but are rather too young when they are sent to the packing station to be seriously affected by any disease." They are given a small amount of antibiotic in their feed to suppress disease.

Fowl pest is the greatest dread of a poultry farmer's life. It can sweep through these intensive units very rapidly, and slaughter of the entire flock on a farm has been compulsory. Compensation was payable by the Ministry of Agriculture.

Apart from fowl pest there is always the risk of mechanical aids going wrong. A broiler manager entered his house one morning and noticed that all was curiously still and quiet. His birds were all dead because his ventilation fans had stopped working. The temperatures of the houses can be controlled upwards by thermostat but not downwards, because refrigeration units would cost too much to install. " I just cross my fingers and hope for the best during a heatwave," the manager told me. " More than a day or two of very hot weather can kill them."

The chickens, after 9 to 10 weeks in these dim, enclosed houses, reach their required weight of 3½ lb. and are caught, crated and sent to the " packing station."

On a visit to one packing station, an innocuous-looking, factory-like building, we were issued with white overalls and wellington boots to protect us from the blood in the slaughter room. Then we went into the shed. Crates were stacked up the inside wall, 12 birds to the crate. The birds are starved for 12 to 16 hours before they reach the packing station and they are apt to spend the best part of a day in their crates after they reach it, before their turn comes. During this time they get neither food nor drink, because any undigested food is waste and can impair the keeping quality of the carcase in the deep freeze.

Taken out of their crates, the birds are suspended by their legs on a moving belt, gently because they must not be frightened or they would not de-feather so well. The time taken to reach the slaughterman varies between one and five minutes according to the layout and speed of the conveyor belt. As they move along their beaks open and shut, mutely, in what has all the appearance of fear, but I was told that chickens are dim creatures and have not the slightest idea of what is happening to them.

More than 200 million birds pass each year through the packing stations. There is no legislation to protect them from having their throats cut while fully conscious. I was informed by the Humane Slaughter Association that of the birds which have their throats cut in full consciousness, two out of five go into the scalding tank alive.

Mr R. A. Wright, M.R.C.V.S., of the Houghton Poultry Research Station, commented in the Association's 1959-60 Annual Report: " I have no hesitation in considering jugular severance without prior stunning as being grossly inhumane as birds were obviously fully conscious and in great pain for some appreciable time."

Some packing stations use " stunners " before the birds have their throats cut; some do not. A packing station I visited had stunners but did not use them. " The birds do not bleed properly if you stun them," said the manager, " it is much quicker our way, and kinder, too."

I watched the birds having their throats cut and disappearing, flapping wildly, into a bleeding tunnel, to re-appear a minute later, still flapping wildly, to go into the scalding tank. " They are dead before they go into that," said the manager reassuringly. When the birds came through the scalding tank they were limp and dead.

They then went through a de-feathering machine and at this point were conveyed past the live birds and through a gap in the wall into the evisceration and packing rooms.

In 1961 some 28 million laying birds —nearly half the total—were housed in battery cages.

In the battery unit automation is exploited to the full. The cages are ranked one above the other, three, four, or even five tiers high. Food is supplied by a conveyor belt and water is laid on.

The bird stands on a wire grid which has a one-in-five slope from back to front, so that the egg rolls away into a rack in front of the cage.

The droppings fall on to a tray which is automatically " squeegeed " off at intervals.

For a long time only one bird was housed in each cage, then two were tried together. Mortality was no greater, and the birds even seemed to enjoy the companionship. Then three birds were tried to a cage; some even tried four to the ordinary 15- or 16-in. cage.

One firm is making production comparisons with " one bird to a 9½-in. cage, two to a 12-in. cage and three to a 16-in. cage. Other possible combinations are four to a 16-in. cage or four or five in a 24-in. cage."

" Stimulighting " was introduced by the Americans a short while back. This was an increase in hours of lighting to stimulate more activity in the pullet and encourage her to lay more eggs. Lights were put on early in the morning and continued late into the night so that at the peak of her laying period the bird could have more than 20 hours' light a day.

But a suspicion has been growing in the minds of British poultry keepers that this overstimulus has caused nervousness and " vices " in the birds. So they have introduced " twilighting," or the dimming of lights in the houses, so that the birds spend their whole lives in perpetual twilight. But although the birds go on laying eggs in the dimness, it is difficult for their attendants to see to do their jobs, so many producers have opted for red lights which can be slightly stronger without " disturbing " the birds.

Recently, however, a curious thing began to happen. The *Farming Express* reported (December 14, 1961): " The sudden death of apparently healthy, strong pullets in battery cages is presenting research workers with a problem. The birds die of heart failure, but neither the cause nor a cure has been found. . . ."

Dr W. G. Siller, of the Poultry Research Centre, Edinburgh, thought that the birds were suffering from " cage layer fatigue." In the paracute form, he said (*Farmer and Stockbreeder*, December 19, 1961), " the birds drop dead." In the acute form " there is prostration . . . the birds will die if neglected, but if hand-fed or nursed they may recover after several weeks or even months." This, the article points out, " is, of course, uneconomical on a farm scale."

The birds most prone to this condition were White Leghorns. Postmortems showed the birds to be normal except for their bones, which were thin and soft. The eggs had been normal, without soft shells.

Increased egg production brings headaches as far as egg quality is concerned. Poor shells, thin shells, pale yolks, watery whites, all prove a problem. For poor shells and thin shells improvement can be made with additions to diet, while emulation of the golden yolked free-range egg can be got by feeding dried grass or, if that proves too expensive, by feeding a yellow dye to the bird.

(Adapted from Ruth Harrison's
Animal Machines)
'The Observer Weekend Review'
1 March 1964

Views on animal factories

Ⓑ Distorted

From Dr D. W. B. Sainsbury, B.Sc., M.R.C.V.S., Lecturer in Animal Health, University of Cambridge.

SIR,—Anyone reading Mrs Ruth Harrison's book, "Animal Machines," and unfamiliar with the true picture of British livestock farming, would obtain a grossly distorted picture of what is *actually* happening. Having seen the way livestock are managed in several foreign countries and comparing these methods with our own, I have little doubt that we show more thought for the well-being of these animals than does any other country in the world.

Mrs Harrison talks of intensive management as though it were new —but we have been practising it in one form or another for hundreds of years. The size of the units and the scale of the enterprises are certainly bigger, and the risks of disease are greater, but the general course of events is that mortality is being reduced constantly, to the benefit of animals and man alike.

Mrs Harrison picks out only the systems that appear to fit her argument and ignores those that do not. For example, only a fraction of one per cent of pigs in this country are fattened under the conditions she describes—though her elementary errors in the description of the so-called " sweat-box " for pigs shows that she has never been in one!

The farmer originator of this system of keeping pigs actually developed it to prevent disease—and therefore suffering—in his pigs, and by applying it carefully he has achieved considerable success. I would willingly supply Mrs Harrison with the plans of a modern " sweat-box " to show that pigs do have separate dunging areas, have adequate room, feed cleanly and lie comfortably. Better still, I could show her some in action.

It is a dangerous untruth to suggest that most of our livestock receive food " doctored " with drugs and hormones. Remarkably few hormones are used. Drugs are used when necessary, as in the human population, to control disease. The inclusion of antibiotics in food to meat-producing stock has never to my knowledge been shown to be of any harm to the human population. Legislative control on the use of all food additives is severe, and correctly so.

Plenty of livestock still forage for their food outdoors, but if it is more economic for us to cut the food and take it to the well-housed animal, how is that going to influence any person or animal adversely ? We try to provide the livestock with comfortable conditions where competition for life is removed. Under outdoor conditions the struggle for existence is sometimes severe, discomfort may be great, and losses may be more, both from disease and from predators. Yet these are apparently the conditions Mrs Harrison wishes to see imposed on our livestock.

I am sorry I have not the space to say more, but I think Mrs Harrison is unaware that her proposals could well cause more suffering in our animals, rather than less!

David Sainsbury

We give here a selection from all the letters (about 320) prompted by our extracts from Mrs Ruth Harrison's book.

Ⓒ Poles apart

Sir -The most revealing comment on "Animal Machines" comes from Sir Harold Sanders, Chief Scientific Adviser to the Ministry of Agriculture, whom you report as saying that " no case has been established for making it an offence *merely* to deprive animals of light, freedom to exercise or pasture." He would, in fact, concede them existence, but not life in any real sense.

It is extraordinary that two completely opposed attitudes towards animals are found in our time. On the one hand we have, for example, the World Wildlife Fund, which exists to preserve wild animals and birds in their natural habitats; while Peter Scott and other naturalists have taught thousands of viewers to observe animals with sympathy, and with respect for their natural rights as living creatures. On the other hand is the attitude which regards animals as profit-making units.

The arguments used to support this attitude are remarkably reminiscent of those for the retention of child labour in the early days of the Industrial Revolution. One suspects that such views carry within them their own nemesis.

Epsom. **Helen M. Simpson**

Ⓓ Changing the law

Sir,—May I express this Society's appreciation of the publicity you have given to Mrs Ruth Harrison's book, " Animal Machines " ?

The R.S.P.C.A. is entirely opposed to all excessively intensive methods of animal husbandry and is striving to discourage the extension of such practices in this country. The view of my council, however, is that under the existing law the Society could not prosecute with any reasonable hope of success, since definite *physical* suffering, within the meaning of the law, cannot be proved.

In 1961 this Society sponsored the Animals (Control of Intensified Methods of Food Production) Bill, which failed to reach Second Reading. It is our firm intention to seek the reintroduction in Parliament of this Bill as soon as opportunity offers. If the Bill becomes law, we will urge the Minister to bring into effect regulations which at least will serve to standardise conditions and to improve them.

John Hall,
S.W.1. Chief Secretary, R.S.P.C.A.

Ⓔ Bled to death

Sir,—Mrs Harrison indicates that in some premises broilers are bled to death without being stunned. This must cause unnecessary suffering. Instruments are on sale which will stun and kill poultry, and at the same time cut the jugular vein.

The Slaughter of Animals Act 1958 requires horses, cattle, sheep, swine and goats to be slaughtered instantaneously, unless they are stunned first by a mechanically operated instrument, or by electricity. An Act of Parliament could impose similar provisions upon the poultry industry without hardship to anyone.

Hoddesdon. **J. F. W. Harrison**

Ⓕ From the 'inside'

Sir,—As one on the " inside " of the poultry industry, my impression of Ruth Harrison's first article was that much of it was inaccurate, and all of it replete with emotive words.

As regards numbers of hens per cage, up to 42 has been tried and currently 20 for one particular make of cage is widely used. Three to five are generally preferred. The number of hens in cages is currently some 27 per cent of all hens. In 1961 the percentage was nearer 20, not " nearly half the total."

No competent producer would use 20 hours' lighting for egg production. The use of artificial lighting is designed to provide an approximation to the natural rise in daylight hours from 8 to 17, as occurs from December to June. The reason is simply to provide the same number of fresh eggs on the breakfast table in all months of the year.

Mortality in cages is not excessive when compared to the mortality rates found in outdoor flocks. On free range, mortality averages 20 per cent over the country and is much higher in many instances. Fowl pest is prominent because the Government tackled the problem ineptly from the start and made it worth while to incur the disease. Now that compensation for slaughter has ceased (Mrs Harrison seems not to be aware of this) and the problem handed back to the poultry farmer, fowl pest will gradually subside.

Eggs produced in cages are markedly superior in cleanliness and in freedom from taint. The " flavour " claimed to be missing is often traceable to a lack of bacterial content and to freshness. Yolk colour is provided by a naturally occurring pigment in the natural food of the hen. This pigment can now be synthesised and is used to reinforce that already present in the hens' food.

This, Sir, is not a defence of cruelty. Farmers who are cruel to their stock are frequently found in the bankruptcy courts. The intensive production of animal food is very old and will never be cruel if properly used. A modern industrial society cannot foist on to food producers the responsibility for the pursuit of cheaper food production and then hypocritically hold up its hands.

Ilminster. **S. P. Cosgrove**

Ⓖ Human standards

Sir,—Your editorial Comment on Ruth Harrison's book misses one essential aspect of these "animal factories." The fact that we are exploiters of animals so long as we are meat-eaters has been accepted since earliest times. Until recently, the animals destined for slaughter were allowed free running lives within the restriction of open-air fields, and were often accepted as companions and friends of men. Chicken-farmers have taken pleasure in watching hens and their chicks, or in the contemplation of a hen enjoying her dust-bath.

This appreciative participation in the lives of animals is often followed or accompanied by a feeling of gratitude and a respect for all manifestations of life. *All* natural human feelings are outraged by broiler-house methods, and our natural feeling of obligation towards animals that contribute to our welfare is deadened. No amount of so-called cheap " luxury foods " can compensate for the ills inflicted on ourselves by lowering our human standards. We are diminished by our own misdeeds.

Petersfield. **E. L. Grant Watson**

Ⓗ Only answers

Sir,—There are only two answers to Ruth Harrison's heavily biased article against intensive food production: (a) Stop eating animal protein; (b) Pay the price for extensively produced food.

Most people are simply not prepared to do either.

Monmouth. **D. J. Bobbett**

Ⓘ Label them

Sir,—There should be a law compelling all battery veal, pork, chickens, eggs, etc., to be labelled clearly as such in the shops.

I am pretty sure that seven out of 10 housewives would then never buy these products, whether from sentimental or from gastronomic reasons.

Shorne. **(Mrs) Sheila M. Mitchell**

Ⓙ Try it on the dog

Sir,—If I keep my dog in a small box with a slatted bottom, tie him with a three-inch rope, deny him light and feed him—say—on bread and jam and benzedrine, I can be prosecuted.

If by doing all this I could show a profit, would my behaviour then become acceptable to the law and to society in general?

Uckfield. **Barbara Willard**

'The Observer' 15 March 1964

School Meals

Introduction

From 'Education in 1965', a report of the Department of Education and Science.

92. The annual return in the autumn showed that some 4,361,040 day pupils were taking school dinners at maintained schools, or 65.36 per cent of the number present (62.2 per cent in 1964 and 59.2 per cent in 1963). There were 14,869 self-contained kitchens (14,234 in 1964) and 13,022 dining rooms and centres received container meals (13,602 in 1964); 244 schools or departments were without school meals facilities (271 in 1964).

93. Information supplied by authorities for a day in the autumn showed that 307,942 children were taking free meals (280,591 in 1964), 7.06 per cent of those taking meals and 4.62 per cent of the total number of children present (6.09 per cent and 4.3 per cent respectively in 1964).

94. A Departmental working party was set up by the Secretary of State in February, 1965, to review the nutritional standards of the school dinner and to consider whether the present type of meal is appropriate to current tastes. Its report was published in January, 1966.*

* The Nutritional Standard of the School Dinner.

Parents whose children do not qualify for free meals pay 1s. per day, but the actual cost of the meal is about 2s. 6d., the difference being paid by the Exchequer. In 1965 the subsidy totalled about £75m. and it is estimated that by 1969-70 it will amount to £113m.

(A) SCHOOL MEALS

MY daughter tells me that she is the only girl in her form who comes home for lunch. She attends a school where a large proportion of the pupils live at a distance, but not all. Quite a few live in the same area as ourselves. My two younger children attend a small village school and they also are about the only ones to come home at midday.

There has been much public interest recently in the case of the child who was kept from school by her mother because the headmaster would not allow her to wipe her cutlery before eating. I could not help asking myself why the mother did not arrange for her daughter to return home for lunch, instead of keeping her from school.

School dinners were originally intended for poor children who were under-nourished. The service was extended during the Second World War when mothers were needed for war work. Women are still required in industry and the professions. Their children and those who live at a distance still need the service.

So do those children whose parents are too poor to provide a nourishing midday meal. What of the rest? Why do mothers who are prosperous take it for granted that as soon as their children start school they automatically stay for school dinners?

The school meals service is greatly overstrained. The shortage of dining space often entails more than one sitting.

Money for education is in short supply. Is it not time that some of the subsidy for the school meals service should be diverted to satisfy more pressing needs? Alternatively, why should not those for whom the school meals service is a mere convenience pay a much more realistic price for the meal? I would be interested to hear the views of other mothers on this subject.—Yours faithfully,

Audrey Whalley.

Taunton,
Somerset.

'The Guardian'
14 March 1966

LETTERS

B I HOPE the letter from Audrey Whalley on school meals (March 14) will strike responsive chords in more influential places than those to which I have access.

For years, with other long-suffering colleagues at various primary schools, I have protested about this pernicious system, which seems to allow a midday meal without question to any child—even when, as I have known personally, he or she may live across the road from school, with a fit and active mother at home every day.

I shall not be satisfied until all primary school meals are supplied only after due consideration of written application from the parents, who should be able to show that real hardship would fall on the child if school meals were not available.

The service is not, and never was, intended as a casual affair for the convenience of mothers who cannot be bothered to provide a meal at midday. At my present school some two thirds to threequarters of the children who regularly stay admit to having a mother at home, and most of them live within a few minutes' walk.

If Mrs Whalley's letter can start something moving somewhere she will have done more for teachers up and down the country than years of resolutions and conference speeches.
—Yours not very hopefully,

Harry B. Taylor.

Bristol.

C

Points from other letters

THE REASON I first asked for my child to have school dinners was that he was such a poor eater and I thought that having meals with other children would help him with his appetite, and this proved largely successful. When recently, because of a fire at school, I fell in with the request to mothers to feed their children at home if possible, I found that my six-year-old was utterly exhausted by having to go to and fro even for a seven-minute walk. Children in general are not quick eaters, and I had to rush my little boy all the time so that he wasn't late for school. I feel that some mothers do allow their children to benefit from school dinners in the interest of the children and not as a means of getting out of this job.—**Sylvia Kesselman,** Kenton, Middlesex.

D

OUR DAILY SCRAMBLE for the school meal begins at 11 55 a.m. Having no dining room, of course, we have to form the desks into tables, get out the cloths and cutlery as quickly as possible and at the same time ensure that the children wash their hands (again in the usual inadequate toilet facilities found in the old village schools). After the meal, which is eaten with the children, the teachers are still on duty, responsible to the authority for the safety of our young charges as they enjoy play in the playground. The usual minor accidents crop up and we assume the role of nurse and doctor, not to mention mediator in the childish quarrels and fights. Do you wonder we sometimes get a bit disgruntled?—*M. Schofield,* Suffolk headmistress.

E

MODERN CHILDREN have many wide interests which cannot all be catered for in the school curriculum and therefore schools have to provide clubs. At the school where I taught until last September, there were each lunch time three or four clubs in process, to say nothing of athletics or games practice and individual children working in classrooms on their own projects. From this point of view, a school meals service is essential.—**Wendy B. J. Williamson,** Truro.

F

COULD THE ANSWER to the overstrained school meals service lie in the provision of school canteens serving soup, hot drinks, salads, cheese, rolls, and fruit, and simple quick dishes cooked on the premises—something of the milk bar style, perhaps? This could provide mid-morning snacks (some of the children leave home very early in the morning) and tea and biscuits for staff and pupils staying late for music lessons, club activities, house meetings and so on. Economic prices should be paid over the counter. Perhaps some sort of grant could be arranged for really needy children.—(Mrs) **E. D. Howden,** Strathkiness, Fife.

G

IT IS TRUE the price of school meals is uneconomic. None the less it is the parents of children who most need this meal who would be hardest hit by raising the price. If we were to introduce any kind of differential payment scheme the administrative problems would be formidable (how do you define "mere convenience"?), the tiresome task of collecting dinner money made more burdensome to the teachers, and the unpleasant shadow of the means test (a very real memory to many parents) would put a further stumbling block in the path of good home-school relations.—**Davida W. Higgin,** Danbury, Chelmsford, Essex.

H

Mrs WHALLEY'S pertinent letter prompts me to inquire by how much school meals are subsidised, and by how much meals on wheels?—*Margaret Woods,* Abergavenny.

'The Guardian'
23 March 1966

I **QUOTE**

—by Dr. M. Sutcliffe, school medical officer in North West Derbyshire, commenting on an increase in the number of children having school meals:—

The school dinners are of special value to those children with poor appetites. It is usually found that a child who refuses to eat at home will enjoy a meal taken in the company of other children with healthy appetites.

'Daily Express'
4 October 1965

Boy takes the lid off school meals

J **By our Correspondent**

A schoolboy, aged 16, at Gillingham, Kent, has written a letter to his local newspaper claiming that school meals generally consist of "hard and tough meat, lumpy potatoes, stringy cabbage, and dishwater gravy."

Other complaints listed by the boy—Malcolm Wright, of Woodlands Road, Gillingham—concern lack of pepper, damp salt, no water, chipped crockery, and "aggressive" women servers. His headmaster has commended his initiative in writing to the local press.

'The Guardian'
13 May 1966

The Great Train Robbery

Introduction

In August, 1963, the Royal Mail, running from Glasgow to London, was held up and robbed on a lonely stretch of track near Linslade, Buckinghamshire. The total sum stolen was £2,631,684, but by the time of the trial—held at Aylesbury early in 1964—£336,534 had been recovered. Of the eleven men who were found guilty of the main conspiracy seven were sentenced to 30 years' imprisonment, two to 25 years, one to 24 years and one to 20 years. The total of 304 years was reduced on appeal to 251.

Before sentencing the first of the accused the Judge, Mr. Justice Davies, said: 'Roger John Cordrey, you are the first to be sentenced out of certainly 11 greedy men whom hope of gain allured. You and your co-accused have been convicted of complicity, in one way or another, of a crime which in its impudence and enormity is the first of its kind in this country. I propose to do all within my power to ensure it will also be the last of its kind; for your outrageous conduct constitutes an intolerable menace to the well-being of society.

' Let us clear out of the way any romantic notions of dare-devilry. This is nothing less than a sordid crime of violence inspired by vast greed. The motive of greed is obvious. As to violence, anybody who has seen that nerve-shattered engine driver can have no doubt of the terrifying effect on law-abiding citizens of a concerted assault by masked and armed robbers in lonely darkness. To deal with this case leniently would be a positively evil thing. When grave crime is committed it calls for grave punishment, not for the purpose of mere retribution but so that others similarly tempted shall be brought to the sharp realisation that crime does not pay and that the crime is most certainly not worth even the most alluring candle. As the higher the price the greater the temptation, potential criminals who may be dazzled by the enormity of the price must be taught that the punishment they risk will be proportionately greater. I therefore find myself faced with the unenviable duty of pronouncing grave sentences. . .'

(A) Sir—Am I one of a minority in feeling admiration for the skill and courage behind the Great Train Robbery? More important, am I in a minority in being shocked by the savagery of the sentences—30 years for a successful theft as compared with a life sentence (12 years at most in practice) for the rape and murder of a child?

If our legal system sentences a man to 30 years for an offence against property, it is not surprising if some of us feel sympathy for the prisoner who escapes, again with skill and courage, from such a sentence.

A great deal is written about prison life in Communist countries. Now we learn that in our own out-of-date, overcrowded prisons a man can suffer solitary confinement for an indefinite time, except for a brief period each day when he is distinguished from his fellow-prisoners by a distinctive dress, that he sleeps, if he can, in a cell with an ever-burning light, observed by warders every 15 minutes.

Is it intended that this treatment should continue over 30 years if the prisoner does not break down and disclose where

A*

17

the money stolen from the Midland and other banks is hidden?

This is very close to torture for the purpose of eliciting information—torture on behalf of our banks is even less sympathetic than torture with an ideological motive. Yours faithfully.
GRAHAM GREENE.
London. W.1.

'The Daily Telegraph'
20 August 1964

(B) SIR—Mr. Graham Greene (Aug. 20) deprecates the savagery of a 30-year sentence with indefinite solitary confinement for those so far convicted of perpetrating the Great Train Robbery, and sympathises with the prisoner who has escaped.

He infers also that because it is bank money that has been stolen the punishment is disproportionate to the crime. Ought he not in defending these thugs convicted and sentenced after a long and fair trial to spare some thought for the engine-driver struck down without mercy during the train robbery, and to the three clearing bank employees who have been killed, and to the 72 injured during the past five years in the far too numerous armed attacks on banks and their staff in charge of cash?

These raids are increasing rapidly, and with the odds against capture and conviction currently quoted at about three to one crime is now paying handsomely, and our members grow daily more apprehensive.

For their greater protection we must therefore press for even more salutary punishment for those convicted of robbery with violence. Unlike Mr. Greene. who does not have to face the risk of being shot or struck on the head by pick-axe handle or iron bar in the course of duty, we can have absolutely no sympathy for the prisoner, nor admiration for his miscalled skill and courage.

Thugs they are, and as thugs they should be treated.
Yours faithfully.
JOHN ELLIS, Chairman.
Central Council of Bank
London, E.C.2.   Staff Assns.

(C) Sir—Crime increases every day: prisons are overcrowded, and only the most repressive and inhuman methods, as Mr. Graham Greene points out, can keep a determined gaol-breaker in. Stealing from a bank secures the severest prison sentence known to the law. The brutal rape and murder of children and the battering to death of old people is comparatively lightly punished.

Obviously the whole penal code urgently needs revision. Try to raise this vital question with either party at the coming election and be prepared for an evasive answer.

I am willing to wager odds on that the first " urgent " legislation likely to occupy the new Government, be it Conservative or Labour, will be increased pay for M.P.s.   Yours faithfully,
London, W.1.   A. S. FRERE.

(D) Sir—Surely the whole point is not that the train robbery sentences were shocking, but that the sentence Mr. Graham Greene quotes for the rape and murder of a child was shockingly inadequate.
Yours faithfully.
EDGAR D. WESTLAKE.
Wilts.

'The Daily Telegraph'
22 August 1964

(E) Sir—Mr. Graham Greene's admiration for the mail-train thugs and their cowardly assault on law-abiding citizens does him little credit.

When he equates the richly-deserved sentences of the train robbers with the admittedly often inadequate punishment of murderers, his is a typical example of the woolly thinking and blind vindictiveness of the Leftist " progressive " with an anti-" Establishment " obsession.

If he were capable of a smattering of elementary logic he would see that the inadequacy of the punishment in one case is no excuse for leniency in the other, and that his complaint is merely a strong argument for bringing the penalties into line by levelling up, not down.

It is his sort of thinking and teaching that is largely responsible for the present crime rate being the highest ever, and his deplorable hero-worship of squalid, cowardly criminals is a major cause of the current appalling level of juvenile delinquency.

It was an appropriate and timely after-comment on his letter that on the following day you published a report concerning Mr. Jack Mills, the injured engine-driver of the plundered train. How its account, if he read it, of 39 weeks of still unfinished hospital treatment and possible permanent disablement, must have filled Mr. Greene anew with admiration for the skill, courage and enterprise of those splendid bandits. Yours faithfully.
G. E. HOWARD,
Farnham, Surrey.   Major.

(F) Sir—In the two cases Mr. Graham Greene takes it is at least possible that the man who attacks a child is suffering from some mental or physical illness. Obviously he should be kept under restraint until it is reasonably certain that he will not do it again.

The others (train robbers) are sane, clever men who think the possible gain is worth the risk. If they do not like a long rest in a prison which is not sufficiently comfortable all that they have to do is to refrain from robbery with violence.   Yours faithfully,
F. A. HARPER
Somerset.

'The Daily Telegraph'
25 August 1964

Maria Marten

Introduction

A dreadful crime has been brought to light at Polstead in this county. The circumstances which have reached us are as follows: Maria Marten, a fine young women, aged 25, the daughter of a small farmer, in the above village, formed an imprudent connection two or three years ago with a young man named William Corder, the son of an opulent farmer in the neighbourhood, by whom she had a child. He appeared much attached to her, and was a frequent visitor at her father's house. On the 18th May last, she left her father's house with William Corder and was not afterwards seen, but when several weeks had elapsed, and no intelligence was received of their daughter, although William Corder was still at home, the parents became anxious in their enquiries. Corder named a place at a distance where he said she was, but that he could not bring her home for fear of displeasing his friends. Her sister, he said, might wear her cloths, as she would not want them. Soon after this . . . Corder resolved on going abroad. Accordingly he left home in September last, expressing a great desire before he left *to have the barn well filled*. Strange surmises lately gained circulation throughout the neighbourhood and one person stated as a singular circumstance that on the evening when Maria disappeared, he had seen Corder enter the Red Barn with a pickaxe. The parents became more and more distressed and unsatisfied and their fears were still more strongly agitated by the mother *dreaming on three successive nights last week*, that her daughter had been murdered and buried in the Red Barn. . . . Strange to say, in the very identical spot which the mother had dreamt of, was found, at two feet underneath the surface, the body of her unfortunate child. . . . The murdered remains were buried on Sunday night, at Polstead, in the presence of an immense concourse of spectators.

[Corder was traced to Brentford, where Constable Lee entered his house by a stratagem and found him]'in the parlour with four ladies, at breakfast. He was in his dressing-gown, and had a watch before him by which he was minuting the boiling of some eggs. . . . The prisoner was transmitted, to abide his fate, to the county gaol of Suffolk'. [Corder was convicted of murder and hanged at Bury St. Edmunds on 11 August, 1828.]

'The Ipswich Journal,' 26 April 1828

Joanna looks in at Maria's cottage

Actress Joanna Van Gyseghem, who plays the title role in the melodrama "Maria Marten, or Murder in the Red Barn", which opened at Colchester Repertory Theatre on Tuesday, visited Polstead last week to have a look at the cottage where Maria lived. Joanna is wife of Ralph Bates, son of Dr. and Mrs. Ralph Bates, of Colchester.

Melodrama of Suffolk Murder

Ⓐ

MORE than 130 years ago East Anglia was shocked and fascinated by the murder of Maria Marten in the Red Barn at Polstead. In contemporary reports one can read that between 12,000 and 14,000 people watched the execution of 24-year-old William Corder at Bury St. Edmunds.

This week the Colchester Repertory Company is performing John English's version of the murder, presented as a Victorian melodrama.

William Corder, the villain who murders his mistress rather than marry her after she has borne his child, is played by Kenneth Poitevin, complete with twirling side whiskers and black clothes. The audience participated by hissing and booing whenever he entered the stage, despite his threatening fists and looks.

FIRST APPEARANCE

Joanna Van Gyseghem makes her first appearance with the company as the ill-fated Maria, and Hans De Vries is the revengeful hero who gets his man in the end.

The company's production is hilariously funny, with stylised actions and appropriate songs. Lionel Thomson is musical director, and also provides the accompaniment during the play. His choice of Victorian music hall songs to fit the plot shows how much work has been put into the teaming of music and play.

'East Anglian Daily Times'
19 January 1966

At the Rep.

Ⓑ **AMUSING**

WHENEVER Colchester Rep. Company see fit to put their tongues firmly in their cheeks the result is a guaranteed abundance of laughter, and the current production of " Maria Marten " is an hilariously set-up example of their talent in this respect.

Despite the bewildering stodginess of an unbelievably stick-in-the-mud first night audience, bent it would seem, on taking the whole thing. desperately seriously — I even suffered the entertaining indignity of being politely castigated for hissing the villain by a charming elderly lady nearby—the cast drew such detailed acting diagrams that by the second act a complete change-round of audience viewpoint had taken place and my elderly lady actually apologised as politely as she had complained and was soon booing, hissing and cheering with the best.

Joanna Van Gyseghem makes the name part an appealingly naive, excellently-timed study in winsome ingenuousness, while Kenneth Poiterin, for all his shaky words, has plenty of wicked charm as the dastardly Corder and Edmund Gray's mouldering ruin of an Ephraim, and Ralph Bates' lively Timothy Bobbins are but two of several performances very much in the right vein.

I had no reservations this time about Robin Archer's settings, which all had a touch of genuine inspiration, rendered the more effective by most apt and often humorous lighting—I loved the bobbing spots—and the old familiar songs made fitting comment on the action generally.

The murder itself, I felt, was too protracted and not really violent enough, and though Maria's body was beautiful enough in all conscience to be worth preserving, a little de-composition make-up would not have come amiss—though I am aware of the time factor.

Generally, however, a vastly amusing and audience-involving evening.

Theatre Critic   L.R.J.
'*Colchester Express*'
20 January 1966

Ⓒ Sir,—After reading the review by your critic on the production of 'Maria Marten' at the Colchester Repertory Theatre, I persuaded some of my family to see it on the last night.

We went with some misgivings about the proprieties of a play that combined the tragically true story of the seduction and subsequent murder of the young Polstead girl by a son of the local 'gentry', with singing and laughter.

Imagine our delight to find the whole production entertaining to a high degree and excellently performed.

Having talked to several friends about this and found that, like us, they have not been to the Colchester Theatre 'for years', I feel that we must have been missing some first-class productions and that this error must be corrected in the future.

(Mrs.) G. M. Knighton, Essex.

'*Essex County Standard,*'
21 January 1966

' Maria Marten '

Ⓓ   To the Editor

Sir,—So the murder of Maria Marten is to be enacted once more within nine miles of the site of the actual tragedy and the company's production is to be "hilariously funny."

I think it is within the bounds of possibility that descendants of the Corder Marten families are still living in the district. I suggest that the cast first goes to Polstead churchyard and reads the pathetic inscription on the tragic row of graves of the Corder family and reads Miss St. John Adcock's passage in "The Warped Mirror" where she imagines Mrs. Corder going to her back door as the church clock strikes noon in a deserted Polstead on the day of the execution at Bury of her last remaining son and quietly murmuring "Well, happen it's all over now" and then think again.

One cannot have loved the places these people once loved and lived in the house where this unfortunate girl once worked without feeling that here true sorrow was and mirth is very much misplaced.

I wonder if one day, a few decades hence, some company will enact the ghastly crimes, which so wring our hearts today, to the hilarious amusement of local audiences.

MARIAN STRINGER
(formerly of Polstead)

'*East Anglian Daily Times*'
22 January 1966

Ⓔ

The following reply to Miss Stringer's letter was written at our invitation by Mr. David Forder, Administrator of the Colchester Repertory Theatre.

This kind of letter is well known to theatre managers. It usually seems to be prompted by the outrage of moral or religious susceptibilities; it is written by someone who does not come to see the object of complaint and does not approach the alleged perpetrators directly; and it is written after the event, no attempt having been made to prevent it.

Three charges, stated or implied, must be answered:

1. Offence may have been caused to Corder or Marten descendants.
2. The play is untruthful.
3. The hilarity of the play is offensive.

1. *Offence may have been caused to Corder or Marten descendants*

One ground for complaint is confused: is it that the revival of such unhappy memories is unbearably moving, or that the events depicted are derogatory?

How long ago must a person have died to make acceptable revelations of his personal life, or his impersonation on stage or film? Surely 140 years is long enough to avoid causing distress to anyone who knew the protagonists of 'Maria Marten'. Why did the Corder family themselves, if any survive, not protest? Did they know of the play's current production? How does the nearness of the production to the scene affect the issue when the play is the most celebrated melodrama of its kind, and has been produced hundreds of times all over the country and several times in Colchester since 1840, the first known date of its production?

One can sympathise with the Corder family's distress in 1828 when a million broadsheets were sold telling of the crime, when over 10,000 people witnessed the public hanging of Corder at Bury St. Edmunds, and when the rope was sold for £1 an inch. But have they, or Miss Stringer, written to the Curator of the Bury St. Edmunds Museum to complain that Corder's skull is on view there to the public, with an account of his trial bound in his own flayed skin? Have they complained to the Rector of Polstead Church that an account of the event is included in the pamphlet on the church on sale there?

2. *The play is untruthful*

Is it possible for a play to tell the truth? Events could not be put on the stage or film just as they occurred. Much of real life is disorganised and boring. Selection is necessary of what is significant and relevant within the terms of a standpoint, perspective and organised shape. My appreciation of the play about Sir Thomas More, 'A Man for all Seasons', is in no way diminished by the knowledge that 'it didn't happen just like that'. To protest would be to confuse truth with accuracy. It is quite acceptable for a play to be based on real events with episodes which are frankly fictitious. A number of historical romances fall into this category.

It is possible to portray on stage or film events which in real life would be unbearable to witness. Scenes of violence in 'cops 'n robbers' films afford pleasurable thrills to the audience. In real life, a witness might be terrified into insensibility. In this way, it might be claimed that a play cannot tell the truth, as it is unlikely that a sophisticated audience will react to it as they would to real life. The mere fact that real life is portrayed on the screen in a documentary or newsreel diminishes its impact. How otherwise, horrified as we were, would we have borne to watch the assassination of President Kennedy? There is some case to be made out here that we are all in danger of loss of sensibility. Nowadays, few of us would be willing to watch a hanging. Can we watch the representation of Corder's hanging on stage without reproach?

In its presentation, was it offered with documentary veracity? This question can be answered only with reference to the conventions of the play—see section 3 below.

The play 'Maria Marten' never set out to tell the events accurately or truthfully. The real Maria was not by all accounts a pure village maiden, but a girl who at the time of first meeting Corder had two illegitimate children. The play romanticises her, and glamourises Corder, allowing him a pathetic scene of repentance and remorse, and a brave death. The untruthfulness of the play, in one sense, so far from being derogatory, is flattering.

3. *The hilarity of the play is offensive*

Comedy was not only permitted but expected in melodrama. There was always a part of the 'low comedian' involving traditional jokes, songs and slapstick of varying relevance to the plot. This play was true to form in that the low comedian 'Tim Bobbin' baited the villain Corder. Much of the fun came from the attempted infringement of the dignity of the villain (never ultimately successful) and gaining point from the fact that the villain was a frightening character, not to be tampered with without danger.

There are possible elements of comedy in a contemporary revival which are not present in a 19th century production; problems arise in reviving defunct conventions, involving reproductions of obsolete style and techniques, and an obsolete scale of values implicit in the play. The melodrama used devices now discredited: 'asides', for instance, and a rhetorical style of acting now thought inflated and bombastic. It also employed ideals now regarded as too simple to be tenable in such form: innocence, heroism, patriotism.

Is it possible to make a complete and faithful re-creation? Conventions are an agreement, to a great extent subconscious, between artist and audience as to the mode of expression and communication. When they become wholly conscious, trouble may start. The conventions of melodrama included, surprisingly to us, intense emotional identification with the action of the audience. They cheered, wept, hissed and cried out warnings. This identification was possible because they accepted with complete conviction not only the conventions but the ideals of the play.

It is almost inevitable that a modern audience will hold simplified values up to ridicule. The only possible technical device in the theatre to mitigate this is the use of music to induce sentiment. Does the last night audience at the Proms really approve of the jingoistic words of 'Land of Hope and Glory' it sings with such fervour?

In a present-day production of a melodrama, the aim must be clearly defined: is it to satirise the values and conventions of the play, or to re-create them as far as possible in modern terms? Our aim was not to satirise 'Maria Marten'. We had affection for it; and we thought that to do so would defeat its own ends by destroying the substance of the play, and by becoming monotonous after the first few minutes, turn out to be unfunny.

The audiences of 'Maria Marten' sometimes took a little time to get the hang of it. It took expert acting and production to direct their response clearly for them. Of course, it was not possible for them to react spontaneously in just the same way as an audience of the 19th century. They enjoyed booing and hissing and cheering with a certain kind of self-consciousness which would not have been present among their great-grandfathers.

There were certain items which would have been taken as pathos by a 19th century audience, the mood of which would have been impossible to reproduce authentically; for instance, the song 'Do Not Trust Him, Gentle Maiden'. This song is now a stock joke, which, like 'Come Into the Garden Maud', could not be expected to be taken more than half seriously even in the concert hall. We took the only course we thought possible: to play these items with the utmost gravity and musical skill. A prime consideration is that it should be possible for the item to fit with emotional integrity into the total context of the situation and the play within its own terms.

Wherever it was possible to achieve pathos, we tried hard for it. Music helped here a great deal. The death of Maria was, according to a number of theatre patrons, surprisingly moving. The repentance of Corder was helped in achievement of style by clear Shakespearean pastiche in the script. The death of Corder was dignified, impressive and pathetic.

Miss Stringer stands condemned on the very charges she levelled at the theatre: of jumping to wrong conclusions through not having taken the trouble to examine the evidence. Had she watched her television, she might have seen the actress who played 'Maria' walking among the Corder graves at Polstead and visiting the Marten cottage (we all went). Had she come to see the play, her fears might have proved groundless, as were those of a correspondent to *The Essex County Standard*.

Boarding and Day Schools

(A) SOME subsequent experiences have been more immediately painful but nothing, no nothing, has been so consistently unpleasant. I am talking about boarding school. Even now, a dozen years afterwards, it looms in dreams: I find myself back there, frustrated, bored, lonely, uncomfortable, and wake to experience a fierce relief at having escaped into adult life. And at the time I did not even know that adult life was going to be so enormously more worth living.

Not, I think, that my boarding school was an especially bad one. Though as undistinguished academically as most small establishments, it was not entirely incompetent. There were various agreeable frills such as play-readings, and some less agreeable ones that added up to a general aspiration toward "gracious standards"—an archaic genteelism (changing for the evening meal, etc.) which decked, most inappropriately, the basic boarding school conditions of unappetising, meagre food, cold rooms, and the lack of privacy or freedom. (These conditions appear to be so widespread as to be generally accepted as part of boarding school life, and indeed it is hard to see how they could be mitigated entirely without schools pricing themselves right out of the market.)

Of course day schools are often just as cold, their dinners nasty, and their regulations and customs arbitrary and accentric—but they are *day* schools, workplaces with no pretensions to supplying home comforts, either physical or emotional. In the evening you leave, as adults leave their office or factory, and return to your own place; you are not expected to don slithery velveteen to eat fish pie in a noisy, grubby refectory before retiring—avoiding an Order Mark for tardiness—to a bedroom shared quite probably with people you do not particularly care for and may even dislike. These are not conditions that any adult would tolerate, unless under the duress of prison or military service, yet those who are subjected to this are vulner-

No ordinary kind of life

BY GILLIAN TINDALL 'The Guardian' 23 May 1966

able children or, most often, precarious adolescents.

This is the basic flaw in the boarding school—that it attempts to combine two irreconcilable functions, efficiency as an educational establishment and the provision of a home. The best known schools both for boys and girls fulfil the first function well and do not kid themselves unduly on their ability to fulfil the second—ever heard of Eton, Gordonstoun, or Cheltenham Ladies' College expatiating on their cosiness, their "homelike atmosphere"?

For private profit

Prospective parents might do well to remember that practically all the smaller boarding schools are, after all, run for private profit. Hence the idea is promulgated that it is *fun* for immature human beings to live in a crowd, deprived of affection and of most of their personal property—a fallacy which has never appealed to the less moneyed classes and which most foreigners of all social levels regard with equal distaste. In fact the prevalent Continental idea that the British are cruel to their young is based largely on this upper-class habit of banishing little boys and only slightly older girls from their homes for two thirds of the year.

Boarding school, so runs the myth, "prepares you for life" and "teaches you to stand on your own feet." It is true that it *may* teach you to dissemble your true nature in order to support life in a grossly artificial community composed of people in the same age and class range and usually of the same sex. Whether this is a useful accomplishment, particularly

for girls, is another matter. Certainly it is no sort of preparation (thank heaven!) for ordinary life.

On a purely practical level, it is self-evident that boarding offers few opportunities for acquiring the social and material skills of twentieth-century living: it relates back, rather, to the home schoolroom world of nineteenth-century childhood, servanted and segregated. Nor can it help in the development of an integrated personality to live a life fragmented between home and institution—alternately neglected and indulged—for the returning visitor in his own home is readily pampered by parents guiltily aware that they are depriving him of home friends and involvements. "Oh he's bored at home now," the cry goes. But why is he? Perhaps because he is no longer allowed a consecutive life there.

There are many other things to be said on the subject—but before anyone writes to assure me that velveteen is now discarded and that at her school girls over the age of thirteen and a half are allowed to go for walks beyond the gates, I must make what seems to me the central point: to hand a child over to the custody of others for the greater part of the year is to renounce, in some measure, one's responsibility as a parent. One *may* have good ulterior reasons for taking this step—distance from a possible day-school, lack of a settled or complete home, etc. On the other hand one may not. It is quite possible to wish to get your small son or daughter off your hands from a mixture of snobbery, self-deception, and straightforward, old fashioned laziness. Let us, at least, be clear about this.

LETTER · SIXTH-FORM PALLADIUM FODDER

(B) WE ARE the Secondary Modern "lay-abouts." We didn't pass our eleven-plus, and, in consequence, we have been classified as future Palladium fodder and transferred to the Accrington brick monstrosities which some benighted architect has decreed should be our schools.

The strange thing is, a phoenix has arisen out of these secondary modern schools. Why, we would not set foot inside a grammar school now that we have had a taste of the stimulating eventful life in a secondary modern school. Our coeducativeness, our variety of home backgrounds, our varied intelligences interact to produce mature and independent girls who are more fit to face the world than your giggly grammar school girls.

From what we hear, the attitudes of the pupils are even reflected in the personality of their teachers. The good secondary modern teacher, the successful teacher, is a friendly humorous person with a knowledge of our television society, and a persuasiveness founded upon insight and tact. Our poorer teachers have a distinctive highbound grammar school flavour, smacking of Queen Victoria, corporal punishment, and "All Things Bright and Beautiful." The worn-out shell of a teacher, due for retirement years back, still churning out the same lessons, soon goes back to the higher regions from whence he came, while the ex-grammar school girl, the new recruit fresh from college, very "green," eager to be liked, afraid to punish the worst mistake for fear of losing popularity, is frighteningly immature.

We don't suppose the readers of the "Guardian" have ever been in our position, where we feel more progressive than our student teachers. It is rather frightening.

And there is another thing. Whether you like it or not, Labour Party assertiveness is here for the next five years and will be reflected in the educational system. The frozen-food-fed children of semi-detached middle-class parents will benefit by coming into contact with the sturdiness, yes, and sometimes the criminality of those less fortunate than themselves. May we give you some advice? If your children are shortly to become comprehensive, do not quail—be patient with their increased loquacity and occasional misdemeanours. At least you will be aware that they have the toughness to withstand the supermarket pressures of 1966.

One final thought. We and our kin are the mothers of the future. Please do not say we are inverted snobs, have chips on our shoulders, and are too brutally aggressive to be fit company for your darling daughters. It is just that we in the ranks would like you to consider our point of view. In 1966 you have to shout hard and long before anyone pays attention.—**Anne Ellis and the six sixth-form girls of Bishop Wulstan School, Rugby.**

'The Guardian'
23 May 1966

LETTERS... boarding schools

(C) THE juxtaposition of your article about boarding schools and the letter from the disgruntled secondary modern school girls (May 23) must be more than a coincidence.

The secondary modern school girls are supposed to be the "underprivileged," but how many boarding school pupils wouldn't change places with them to gain more freedom, even if it meant a lowering of academic standards? I continually meet sixth-formers to whom the boarding school myths of self-reliance have worn a bit thin. But the real tragedy lies in the number of boys and girls, especially girls, who are miserably unhappy at their schools, but who haven't the courage to tell their parents because of the financial sacrifices they are making to send them there in the first place.—Yours faithfully,

John Brown.

Richmond, Surrey

(D) POOR GILLIAN TINDALL! She hated her boarding school so much that now she can't think straight about the subject at all. It doesn't suit all children, and clearly it didn't suit her, and she might have been happier at home. But she really mustn't close her eyes to the fact that there are many who did, and do, enjoy boarding school.

Some children are ready for a measure of independence before they leave school, and gradually to renounce one's authority over one's children and allow them to create a life of their own is part of a parent's job. Sometimes this hurts, and any parent who has felt the pang occasioned by tidy, empty bedrooms at the beginning of term knows that it does. It is not always snobbery or laziness which prompts this sacrifice.

The best springboard for this plunge into independence is the certainty that home is there, unchanged, reliable, and welcoming.

It is not clear what she means by the "cosiness" which she values so much; most youngsters, in my experience, don't care overmuch about the soft furnishings; and if it is emotional cosiness she has in mind, this sounds very much like the very thing we wish to avoid. More damage and unhappiness are caused by breathing down one's children's necks than by standing back a little and watching them grow.

If boarding schools habitually turned out grumbling misfits and day schools produced uniformly stable and cheerful individuals, we should have to think again.

To allow one's children to attend even day school is to renounce, in some measure, one's responsibility as a parent. Or does she want us all to be Joy Bakers?

Marian Souster.

Felixstowe, Suffolk.

(E) MANY PARENTS of this generation who themselves suffered the physical and emotional deprivations of boarding school life have hesitated to perpetuate the pattern with their own families. There seems little doubt that children educated from home are socially and emotionally more mature than their boarding school counterparts.

However, I would like to point out some of the difficulties of bringing up a "day school" family. They see their parents daily reacting to all kinds of stresses and strains, which is a desirable thing, but it does mean that the parents have little relief from the tug of war of family and professional life. The recent decision to levy a tax on domestic workers throws into relief the problem of the mother with all her children at home.

Mothers of day-school children may not suffer from "a mixture of snobbery, self-deception, and . . . laziness." They tend to be overworked and under-privileged. I wonder if there will ever be a Government enlightened enough to improve this situation.—Yours faithfully,

Rose Haeffner.

Exeter, Devon

(F) HAVING thoroughly enjoyed boarding school myself from the age of 11-16, I was keen to let my own four children have the benefit of the experience. However, after reading many remarks like Gillian Tindall's, I wondered if perhaps children had changed radically since I was a girl. So I gave my children the opportunity of deciding after one term. They decided unanimously in favour of staying at their boarding school, and in fact, the youngest, who was then not 7, made such a fuss about being kept at home that I eventually allowed him to go too.

If anyone feels deprived, it is certainly not the children. I am the one who feels deprived, as I like my children's company.—Yours sincerely,
(Mrs) **Corinne de Roeck.**

London NW 3.

'The Guardian'
1 June 1966

EDUCATION

Secondary Modern Children

(G) KATHLEEN GIBBERD

☐ When schools are merged to form comprehensives all the vocal anxiety is on behalf of the grammar schools. But what about the good secondary modern where the staff have bent all their faculties to devise the right sort of education for Newsom children? It is equally important that these standards also shall be preserved. Consider, for example, a small London school for boys which is due to amalgamate with a grammar school in 1970. Taught by conventional methods, the children here would endure their school days with resentment or boredom. In fact this was the picture two years ago. Then a new head and willing staff collectively set about kindling creative ability and thereby self-confidence. You see the results in pictures and verses on the walls and in models on the shelves – but even more in the faces of the children. There are other devices. There is a crash programme for backward readers. There are conduct sheets where past delinquencies can be erased for ever and new records built up for future employers. In the woodwork shop they mend the broken equipment personally collected from a neighbouring centre for young spastic children. Once a week some local man comes to the school to describe his job - anyone from a garage hand to an Anglican parson. The headmaster says it is a mistake to think that children of indifferent intellectual ability are deficient in other qualities. They have plenty of imagination, he says, and 'they are shrewd and know quite well when a teacher cares about them'. Is he worried about the amalgamation? No, he thinks it will be good for his boys because it will remove the sense of rejection. But I wondered if he was assuming that they would continue to have the right teachers. He keeps losing good men because the special London allowance is totally inadequate for the excessive cost of a home in or near SW3 – especially for men on the basic scale.

☐ This is one kind of secondary modern school – and one in keeping with the original intention. Much more common is the kind that follows the grammar school pattern. Dishonest thinking pretends that such a school gives the same opportunities as a grammar school so long as it provides GCE courses and a transfer to grammar school for those who achieve enough O-levels. Up to 1963 (no later figures available) the proportion of graduates in secondary modern schools was 17 per cent, as against 77 per cent in grammar schools and 42 per cent in comprehensives. I can find no evidence that the figure has risen much. Bournemouth, for instance, gives 20 per cent, including graduate equivalents.

'New Statesman'
3 June 1966

Agricultural Sprays

FIVE MADE ILL BY POISON IN STREAM

Ⓐ

CROPS SPRAY

DAILY TELEGRAPH REPORTER

FIVE people became ill after a poisonous crop spraying chemical infected their water supply. All suffered from severe stomach cramp and muscle pains.

One of the affected people, Mr. John Mawhood, 33, a weed spraying expert, claimed last night that the chemical could kill humans. No antidote has yet been found for it, he said.

The chemical was being sprayed on crops at Woodborough, Notts., when several gallons were accidentally spilled into a stream. The stream provides water to nearby houses.

Fish die

The five ill are Mr. Mawhood, of Old Mill House, Woodborough, his wife Mary, 25, and neighbours Mr. Keith Rowbottom, 29, his wife Dinah, 26, and George Hunt, a farmworker.

Hundreds of fish in the stream, including trout, have died. Cattle have also become sick from drinking the poisoned water, which could prove fatal to them, said Mr. Mawhood.

The stream, which runs through Woodborough to the River Trent, is a favourite haunt of children. So far no children have reported feeling sick.

'The Daily Telegraph'
10 September 1963

CROP-SPRAY DANGERS

Risks to Humans from Chemical Poisons

Ⓑ

SIR—How many of your readers noticed your report on Sept. 10 of the five people being poisoned by a crop-spraying chemical which had polluted the stream at Woodborough, Nottinghamshire, from which they drew their water supply? As a result hundreds of fish in the stream, which runs into the River Trail, have died. Apparently the chemical could kill humans, but there is no antidote for it.

This is not an isolated incident of crop spraying. Poisoning of this sort in one chemical form or another is going on all over the country, destroying wild life indiscriminately and affecting human life in varying degrees. Very little research is being conducted on the effect these sprays are having on the ecology of the country or on the health of individuals. It is surely time that official quarters awoke to the seriousness of the situation.

To those who doubt the dangers of this wholesale method of chemical extermination, may I recommend Miss Rachel Carson's book "Silent Spring"? This work can leave one in no doubt as to the crimes which are being committed in the name of progress.

Yours faithfully,
R. J. F. PHILLIPS.
Esher, Surrey.

'The Daily Telegraph'
12 September 1963

Hampshire Salmon Deformities

Radio-Activity Risks?

Ⓒ Sir—You published a letter from Mr. Alex W. Jardine, on June 1 commenting on the problems raised by salmon deformities which had been observed in the Hampshire Avon, and suggesting the possibility that this could be due to man's interference with nature.

The International Society for the Protection of Animals has been in contact with the Bergen Aquarium on this matter, but unfortunately they cannot comment on the abnormal salmon fry in Hampshire owing to their lack of specific information. Abnormalities in salmon fry are comparatively common and it is more than likely that the eggs although laid by three or four different females were fertilised from sperm from one single male.

In that case, it could be that this particular male carried the factor of abnormality in its sperm cells thus causing the defects that were observed. At the same time, it must be said that this can only be a deduction.

The effects of contamination by chemical residues on wild life have been vividly reported by Dr. Rachel Carson in "Silent Spring." Little is yet known of the effects of the constant build-up of radio-activity.

Can we afford to ignore the argument that the deformities observed in the Hampshire Avon salmon may have been caused by these effects and not by a natural sperm cell factor?

It is reported that the American Government have in mind a plan for the wholesale harvesting of the sea. It could be that these effects will render such a plan abortive even before it begins.

Yours faithfully,
K. R. C. PRIESTLEY.
Major.
Chief Administrator. International Soc. for the Protection of Animals.
London, S.W.1.

'The Daily Telegraph'
6 September 1963

Ⓓ Sir—I noted with interest the letter from Major K. R. C. Priestly (Sept. 6) on the Hampshire salmon deformities. On the following day you reported a scarcity of crabs at Cromer.

Information in Miss Rachel Carson's "Silent Spring" suggests to me that the salmon deformities and the shortage of crabs may well be due to similar causes, namely contamination by chemical residues.

I see no reason to doubt the correctness of the facts in Miss Carson's book. Man is busy poisoning his own environment, and the ultimate risk is the end of all life on this earth.

It is my view, which I believe to be shared by many people, that the most stringent control of all chemicals must be applied at once. Any delays are serious and long delay may well prove disastrous.

Yours faithfully,
R. W. HARRISON CLARKE,
Llangollen   **M.B., CH.B.**

———

Ⓔ Sir—The five people made ill by chemical weedkiller near Woodborough would receive full compensation from third-party insurance had they been injured by a car of equally reputable make, driven by the man who dumped the substance in the river. They have, however, no more protection than if they had received injuries assisting the police, or were victims of criminal violence.

The obsession of Parliament with sex and trivialities has prevented promised legislation to deal with the last two injustices, but the increasing number of insecticide and weedkiller accidents suggests that all chemicals for farm, home or garden use should carry third-party insurance to pay for the consequences of "driving" them to the public danger.

Substances of known safety, such as sodium chlorate weedkiller, or pyrethrum and derris insecticides, would need no insurance, while substances whose makers disclaim all liability in tiny letters on the tin would be charged like sports cars to cover the risk.

Yours faithfully,
LAWRENCE D. HILLS,
Hon Sec., Henry Doubleday Research Assn.
Braintree, Essex.

'The Daily Telegraph'
12 September 1963

Village "Uproar" Over Spray

"Could" Be Poisonous

Ⓕ Sir—In East Anglia nowadays crops are sprayed from aeroplanes. This summer, whilst newspapers were full of accounts of the use of poison gas in the Yemen, our village council estate was in an uproar after being drenched by a plane spraying sugar beet with what the authorities later admitted "could" be poisonous spray. All had soft fruit and lettuces in their gardens at the time, and several people felt sick and giddy later.

This sort of thing happens frequently in East Anglia now, but unless one can actually prove that the illness is caused by spray nothing can be done. Also, naturally enough, the people affected are often employed by the farmers who have contracted for the spraying, and they do not want to risk their jobs by complaining.

One is also appalled by the number of people who use terribly poisonous "aids" to gardening, and who squirt DDT inside their homes.   Yours faithfully,
JOAN M. SNELLING.
Ludham, Norfolk.

Ⓖ Sir—Mr. Lawrence D. Hills suggests (Sept. 12) that all persons poisoned by the chemical weedkillers should be covered by third-party insurance.

Surely the proper remedy is to forbid the use of these poisons, or, better still, to forbid the manufacture of them. I have gardened for 40 years without the use of either chemical manures or poison sprays, and, owing to the difficulty of getting it, very little animal manure. But by saving all my organic wastes I can still grow as good crops as most people.

If the C.N.D. people would take up the matter and do a little squatting in Whitehall I should be delighted to join them. The appalling danger of this wholesale poisoning of the soil and water is in my opinion as great as the nuclear menace, and should be dealt with at once by the Minister of Agriculture.

Yours faithfully,
Hinckley, Leics.   D. J. GINNS.

Ⓗ Sir—A man in this village lost all his bees as a result of crop-spraying. When he complained to the Ministry he was told that his bees had been trespassing.

Yours faithfully,
M. L. MANNOCK.
Great Easton, Essex.

'The Daily Telegraph'
16 September 1963

Ⓘ CHEMICAL SPRAYS

Sir—May I plead for such public support as will ultimately force manufacturers of household insecticides, disinfectant powders, "air fresheners," moth blocks, etc., to state the active ingredients of their preparation on the outside of the container?

This is rarely done at present, except in the case where the active ingredient is based on pyrethrum.

Thus the family doctor gets nowhere if he asks: "Is any substance containing 'X,' 'Y' or 'Z' used in the house?" The householder in most cases cannot tell him. Indeed, it has been my experience that if one writes to a manufacturer asking whether his product contains, say, para-dichlor-benzene or ortho-di-chlor-benzene, no reply or an evasive one is received in many cases.

The first-mentioned chemical is now almost everywhere, in beetle poisons, in fly sprays, in lavatory blocks, in " fresh air " sprays, in cleaning powders and polishes. Its horrible vapour has a most disturbing effect on those susceptible to it, and recovery after a long exposure takes a considerable time.

Yours faithfully,
JOHN S. BARRINGTON.
Oxford.

'The Daily Telegraph'
3 December 1963

Town sprayed with poisonous chemical

Ⓙ   Argyle, July 7

More than three hundred people have had to leave their homes in Argyle, Minnesota. after a light plane had accidentally sprayed the town with poison.

Atrophine, an antidote to the poison, was sent from Minneapolis. The 500 people who stayed on were told to hose down trees, lawns, and shrubs to make the community safe to live in.

The aircraft, sent to spray the area against mosquitos. made three passes last night before it was discovered it was sending down a shower of parathion. an insecticide described as quite a lethal poison which can be absorbed through the skin. But it is believed that it was not in a concentration strong enough to cause serious harm.—Reuter.

'The Guardian'
8 July 1966

Ⓚ## Gardening Notes

IT is good to see that in the great national drive for scientific advance, the garden has not been overlooked (writes Japheth Slugthorpe, Britain's most progressive gardening correspondent). In 1963 there have been more technological strides than ever towards trouble-free gardening.

Most sundriesmen now stock the new wonder chemical Multi-chlorophenylmethaldehyde sulphate-X, better known by its trade name " Dahlia Death." This not only cleared my borders of dahlias and all other plant life in two

days, but it turned my lawn, 50 yards away, interesting shades of blue, and then saffron, before the grass burst into flames and finally shrivelled into a soggy black mass suitable for compost.

Thanks to the revolutionary new " Plastigarden " kit, I have now gone over entirely to instant clip-on plastic flowers. This autumn, while my neighbours have been going through the tedious ritual of bulb planting, digging over and spreading compost, I still have the dazzling show of daffodils and crocuses which has been admired by all since the spring.

Some readers have written about the reluctance of birds to perch in plastic trees. They are more fortunate than I. Birds filled my garden with the irritating chatter for years, until I smeared " Birdigo," a mixture of trinitro-benzylnaphtha-B and sodium chlorate on all walls, footpaths, fences and branches. The birds spun drunkenly, vomited and screeched away, never to return. Except, that is, for the double-beaked lesser spotted dotterel, which not only seems to thrive on " Birdigo," but uses it to fashion its nest among my carboys of soil solvent.

'Peter Simple'
'The Daily Telegraph'
3 December 1963

Reporting Violence

Introduction

The discovery of a young girl's body buried on a Pennine moor led to a highly publicised trial, in December, 1965, which became known as 'the Moors Trial'. After the investigation of what were regarded as three particularly brutal and sadistic murders, Ian Brady and Myra Hindley were found guilty of murder and sentenced to life imprisonment.

Much of the trial was reported in considerable detail in the Press, and in particular a long description of the protracted killing of 17-year-old Edward Evans, who was battered to death with an axe, drew protests from the public.

Sir,—Because of a current court case, an epidemic of sadism is sweeping across acres of the national newsprint.

There are broadly two views about this. One, derived vaguely (and wrongly I believe) from Freud, has it that violence in mass media satisfies through fantasy an unconscious need for violence and makes us less likely to act violently in real life. The other view is that violent conduct is subject to the laws of learning. This view, I believe, has the most experimental support and I quote in particular the annotated bibliography, "The Effects of Television on Children and Adolescents," prepared by W. Sehramm for Unesco in 1962. Among a mass of data on the social learning of aggression is a crucial experiment by Berkowitz in which groups of college students were shown a film of a man being brutally beaten. Some had been provoked and angered by the experimenter before seeing the film, which did *not* relieve their aggressive feelings; indeed, these were increased by the film.

It is accepted that suicide can be imitative, and so can murder according to police evidence to the Royal Commission on Capital Punishment (1953).

The newspapers' claim that this kind of reporting alerts parents to hazards and therefore saves lives seems to me hypocrisy at its most extreme. And surely, though it may make some parents cautious, will not this reporting make many people unnecessarily nervous if not neurotic? Is it good to increase the community levels of fear and hate? Are these not indeed the emotions which in turn breed sadism? Many feel that there is too much fear about already and complain that friendliness, trust, charity, love, receive too little notice.

Newspapers say they are meeting a public demand. Do many people *really* want to read all this stuff? Are not the newspapers just afraid to let rivals get one up on them?

Though, to me, the trend of evidence is clear, no one can yet prove this thing for certain. But I put it to the purveyors of news —as to purveyors of food and drugs—that the onus is on them. They should prove that seemingly noxious products do no harm, or else keep them off the market. I predict that in 20 years this type of reporting, page after page of murder and mayhem, will seem as obsolete and barbaric as public hangings at Tyburn.—Yours etc.,

Richard Fox,
Consultant psychiatrist.
Severalls Hospital,
Colchester, Essex.

'The Guardian'
21 April 1966

HEADLINE DOCTOR

Ⓑ

ONCE AGAIN Dr Richard Fox, of Severalls Hospital, gains the headlines by attacking the headline-writers.

A newspaper is a mirror, reflecting life as it is, not as the idealist would like it to be. We do not believe everything is for the best in the best of all possible worlds. There is a darker side which must be acknowledged before it can be improved.

Vicious murders *do* happen. Children *are* lured into danger by the handful of psychopaths Dr Fox talks about. Parents are entitled to be told of these things so that they can take precautions, and it would be a poor newspaper which failed to give them this warning.

Dr Fox says that detailed reporting of violence can increase the anxieties of those who tend to be anxious. What he does not say is that the same report can also put potential victims on their guard.

Closed eyes and blocked-up ears were the scandal of the 18th and 19th centuries, when injustice and cruelty were hidden until the reformers — many of them newspapers — tore away the veil of complacency. In the same way, pretending the Moors murder case is not there will not make it go away.

'Essex County Standard' 6 May 1966

When the Press holds up a distorting mirror

Ⓒ

YOUR editorial comment last week seems to support the lengthy reporting of sadism on the grounds that the Press must hold up a mirror to the world. Perhaps so, but need it be a distorting mirror? If the Press was sincerely interested in preventing child-killing it might show a sense of proportion.

Since the Moors trial first reached court probably 400 children under 15 in this country have been killed by motor cars; and two or three by strange men — perhaps none. Chaotic families, whose children are most at risk, are least likely to exert greater control as a result of a press campaign. But accidental death is eminently open to public campaigns and preventive legislation.

During the period covered by the trial, however, press campaigns against other forms of child-killing have not been noticeable apart from the "Daily Mail" which has written about accidental self-poisoning — quite a large cause of death.

To write 15 blood-curdling column-feet on the Moors trial, as the "Evening Standard" did about one day of the preliminary hearings, is to make too much of the mental distortions of an isolated pair of sadistic psychopaths. One is driven to presume that the Press only wants to save children killed sensationally.

RICHARD FOX
MB, MRCP, DPM
Consultant Psychiatrist
**Severalls Hospital,
Colchester.**

'Essex County Standard'
13 May 1966

Harry Whewell

Murder in the press

Ⓓ

THE MOORS TRIAL in Chester this week has brought the expected protests about newspaper coverage of murder trials. Much of what the protesters say about crime being imitative seems to me fairly convincing, and I am totally convinced by their argument that the more some people read of violence, the duller their reaction to violence itself becomes.

But I wonder if they are attacking the wrong target. Instead of arguing that the newspapers should not publish reports of Court proceedings involving sadism, violence, and perversion, should they not be saying that nothing should be published about such cases *except* newspaper reports of the Court proceedings ?

I do not believe that it would ever be possible to enforce either proposition, but if it were I think there might be more to be said for enforcing the second rather than the first.

As things stand, cases like the moors case, or the Christie case, or the A6 murder become the subjects of millions of words in the newspapers and on the radio and television while the trial is on, and then of millions more in newspapers, on radio and television, plus books and magazines when the trial is over.

While the trial is on, what can be said or written is very strictly controlled by the laws of contempt of Court. Only what is said in Court can be used, and not all of that. But when the trial is over the floodgates are opened, and colour and comment and conjecture can take over from hard tried fact.

Growing trend

IF POTENTIAL SADISTS and other perverts can be pushed over the brink by what they read in the straightforward, ungarnished version of a case as reported in a newspaper, how much faster and further can they be pushed by a deliberately coloured and dressed-up version published after the trial in the same newspaper, or in a magazine or a paperbacked book ?

Of the making of books and articles and plays and films from any celebrated case there is no end. Moreover, the trend is growing. These books, plays, and films are read and seen by infinitely more people than could ever have read the newspaper reports of the trials.

In the United States in the 1920s a young boy was murdered by two college students who set out to commit the perfect crime — perfect because motiveless. Through it at least one book and a celebrated crime has become known to millions of people all over the world. If knowledge of its horrific details were confined to those who read the contemporary newspaper reports these details would hardly hold a place in the memory of more than a few thousand Americans.

Of course, some of the books written about celebrated crimes and some of the television programmes and newspaper articles about them have a serious purpose. In the controversy about capital punishment most of the murders of this century have been cited as evidence by one side or the other. Here the factual contemporary newspaper report seems to me the most important weapon in the armoury or argument. When I read a letter in my morning paper on some aspect of crime or punishment which begins: "As was clearly demonstrated in the Christie case. . . ." I am totally unequipped to assess what follows unless my paper reported the Christie case at the time.

Nation harmed

NO PROBLEM that besets our society is more disturbing or baffling than the persistence and increase of violent crime. Not only are the victims of these crimes harmed or destroyed, but the whole nation is damaged and corrupted. Poverty and deprivation and inequality and many of the other things that were once thought to cause it are diminishing, so now we must look deeper for the roots.

Much thought and discussion and research is going into attempts to find these causes. More argument and controversy are needed, but these things rarely flourish around any subject about which information is restricted or suppressed. There may be risks in suppressing nothing that is relevant, but I think the risk is worth the taking.

And of all the information which is relevant to the discussion, the plain newspaper report of the case is the most available and the least polluted. Let anyone who can damp the colour and the conjecture, but the facts are the evidence it is everyone's right to have and, indeed, I would suggest, their duty to read.

'The Guardian'
23 April 1966

The Whole Truth?
MAGNUS TURNSTILE

(E) Whatever else Ian Brady and Myra Hindley may have done, this strange couple could well have hastened the end of two unhallowed freedoms of the British press. For also on trial at Chester are the way our newspapers report such cases and the methods a minority have used to secure the 'exclusive full story' for publication after the verdict. Foreigners have always been shocked in the past to find that the polite, docile, gardening, animal-loving British enjoyed nothing better than a juicy murder case. But public disquiet at all levels about the nature of the published evidence in the Moors case and the revelation that the *News of the World* has been paying the chief prosecution witness for the last six months may well force parliament to look into the desirability of curbing freedoms that have been made to look more like licence, unless the press itself does something about it.

In recent years the press has tended to rationalise its practice of giving all the gory details by supporting the cathartic theory advanced by some psychiatrists: that reading about violence and killing gets dangerous tendencies out of our system harmlessly. Now, however, it is faced with the National Association for Mental Health campaign against verbatim reporting on the grounds that this may encourage the mentally unbalanced to commit imitative crimes. Newspapers will be fooling themselves if they assume this is just another busibodies' movement: whether it is because we have matured since the days when the nation seemed to stop work to read about the Heath, Haigh and Christie affairs; or because the emancipated new generation is too busy living life to need this kind of catharsis (the *News of the World*'s 2 million drop in circulation in a dozen years seems to suggest this); or simply because the reports of the preliminary hearings shocked even hardened homicide fans, the signs are that the Moors trial is having a chastening effect on our *mores*.

One gets plenty of support for this belief in pub, bus and train – 'I've stopped reading the case – it's too horrible.' But perhaps the most striking evidence comes from what might once have been regarded as an unlikely source, the *People*, which last Sunday, under the headline . . . Even The Ghouls Stayed Away', reported that the morbidly curious crowds who normally gather for murder trials were conspicuously absent in Chester.

Fleet Street on the whole has not treated the case with the uninhibited enthusiasm it displayed for the big cases of the Forties and Fifties, but in space terms the first week's coverage showed that it still clings to the belief that a 'good' murder trial, like a general election or a test match, is a useful if temporary circulation-booster. Here is the score in column-inches (the column of a full-sized newspaper is about 21-22 inches long and I have converted the two tabloids' measurements for a more accurate comparison): *Express*, 690; *Sun*, 464; *Sketch*, 418; *Mirror*, 398, *Mail*, 375; *Telegraph*, 373; *Times*, 316; *Guardian*, 276.

However, the bare figures alone are misleading. For instance, a lot of the *Express* space – as much as a third – was taken up by headings alone, while the qualities devoted most of their space to tightly-packed text. But in presentation terms the *Express* has exploited the case more than any of its rivals – it led the front page with the story for the first two days and has spread the report of the proceedings across two pages most days. The only other paper to lead with the case was the *Mirror* (on the first day). It was the *Mail*, however, that stooped to a 'human/glamour' angle. One of its best writers, Vincent Mulchrone, was given the unenviable task of injecting 'colour' into the macabre scene. He wrote: 'Myra Hindley, 23, who had a new ash-blonde rinse, played cat's cradle with her long fingers. When she made notes she replaced her ballpoint pen precisely on her pad, like the efficient shorthand-typist she is.' Her skirt, he reported, 'was a fashionable three inches above her knees'. And *The Times* was the only paper to give a long extract from the transcript of the tape-recording which some of the others described as 'too harrowing' to publish.

Differences of make-up styles tend to give the impression that the less responsible popular papers are playing up the trial while the qualities confine themselves to a toned-down version. But the space given to Smith's detailed and grisly evidence about the alleged hatcheting to death of Evans – presumably the kind of reporting most likely to affect potential imitators – provides an interesting commentary: the *Sun* gave 16 inches of this evidence and led its report with it; next came the *Telegraph* with 14½; *Times*, 12; *Mirror*, 10; *Mail*, 8; *Guardian*, 7; *Sketch*, 5½; *Express*, 5¼.

The fact that the *Express*, while devoting more space to the trial than other papers, has managed to sub-edit the most gruesome evidence down to a third of that printed by another paper indicates that it should not be too difficult for the press to meet the plea of Dr Richard Fox, psychiatrist member of the NAMH, for an 'agreement among editors to exercise some form of self-restraint'. If newspapers fail to act voluntarily, individual editors may yet find themselves facing penalties which would subsequently inhibit the press in the same crippling way as the present libel laws. As my colleague, C. H. Rolph, points out, editors have been lulled for years by the non-enforcement of statutory provisions which successive law officers have been content to hold in reserve. Possibly the most dangerously false sense of security in the prevailing one in Fleet Street based on a misreading of the Judical Proceedings (Regulation of Reports) Act 1926, passed as a result of the 'non-access' evidence in the Russell divorce action. This Act is widely believed by editors to restrict only divorce reports, but it specifically outlaws the printing or publishing 'in relation to *any* judical proceedings' of 'any indecent matter or indecent medical, surgical or physiological details, the publication of which would be calculated to injure public morals.' (It just happens to be conveniently more specific about matrimonial cases, for it tells an editor exactly what he *may* publish concerning them.)

Before any judge finds it necessary to remind editors of this fact in a salutary way the press should jettison all the cant about 'censorship' and 'freedom to tell the whole truth' and acknowledge that a principle that is valid for divorce can be applied to murder trials. Giving up the freedom to report blood-chilling evidence is surely a small price to pay to avoid the danger of even one imitative psychotic copying someone else's crime.

'New Statesman'
29 April 1966

(F) The Whole Truth?

Sir, Magnus Turnstile, commenting on the trial for murder of Ian Brady and Myra Hindley, suggests that newspapers should have reported in much less detail the acts alleged against the accused, calling in aid the view of a psychiatrist that certain psychotics might be led to copy them.

I should like to see some evidence put forward in support of this particular one before I accepted it. And if indeed there are psychotics at large who might be tempted by a newspaper report to commit murder they must be very dangerous people indeed and it would surely be better on all counts to confine them in a place of safety than to censor the newspapers, particularly as the censorship would have to be so far-reaching. If the reporting of murder cases may lead to murder, presumably the reporting of rape cases may lead to rape, of robbery cases to robbery, of assault cases to assault, and so on down the line. Why indeed confine the censorship to newspaper reports? Logically it should surely be extended to novels (Ian Fleming and Agatha Christie have been sources of dangerous corruption for far too long) and plays (what price the Theatre of Cruelty?), and thence into every other sphere.

But the real objection to this kind of censorship is surely one of principle; for those who are denied access to truth or reality are to that extent diminished. Censorship presupposes that there are some people who can be trusted with knowledge and others who cannot, and that the first group can be trusted not only with knowledge itself but also with the right to deny it to the second group.

It is of immense concern to mid-20th century man to know the things of which his fellow men are capable, and thus to understand how precarious are man's defences against his own savagery. If any of those who read these reports can accept the acts alleged as human acts, and their alleged perpetrators as human beings, they will have gained an insight into the nature of man which is intrinsically valuable and which may of itself go some way towards purifying that nature. The opportunity thus presented is one which few may take but all should have.

R. T. OERTON

Poole, Dorset

'New Statesman'
6 May 1966

(G) Sensationalism in BBC news

Sir,—In its news programme, BBC Television has lately made a practice of including, often as principal features, filmed reports of minor disasters of various sorts, especially accidents involving death or injury to a small number of people. Such reports often entail the vivid presentation of suffering on the screen. It would be interesting to know exactly what newsworthy element the BBC sees in material of this kind. Since these items, which have little significance on any national scale, are rarely accorded any comparable importance in the newspapers, one must infer that the differentiating factor is to be found in the more startling (and often sickening) effect of televised news.

Surely the main criterion should be public importance and not the emotive effect to be gained from these intrusions into the world of private suffering. That is to say, it would seem to me right to show film of the suicide of a Buddhist monk or of racial violence in the U.S.A., because the essence of such events is political and of general relevance; but what function is served by an on-the-spot report from a minor aircrash, the effect, as recently, heightened by the panic-stricken cries of injured and onlookers? Does not this appeal merely to morbid curiosity, the same tendency which induces crowds to gather at any accident on the road?

If sensationalism has any meaning, it would seem to be defined particularly well by the BBC's attitude in according items of this solely traumatic nature pride of place in its national bulletins. We do not expect from a body in the presumably responsible position held by the Corporation any sort of cheapness; how much less, then, can we condone that aspect of sensationalism in which the shocking element in personal tragedies is prostituted to the demands of perverse inquisitiveness, often without regard to the feelings of those involved and their friends!

Yours, etc.,

Stevenage

GORDON DAVIES

'The Listener'
7 July 1966

Remembrance Days

VICAR DEFENDS USE OF ATOM BOMBS AGAINST JAPANESE

Ⓐ 'Outrage' Myth Deplored at Armistice Day Service

THE dropping of atom bombs on Japan, and the uprooting of commemorative Japanese cherry trees planted in Ipswich last year, were defended by Canon R. C. R. Godfrey, vicar of St. Mary's, Bury St. Edmunds, during an Armistice Day service at his church yesterday morning.

Canon Godfrey, who was a prisoner of war of the Japanese, said that over the last few years there would seem to have sprung up a kind of myth or legend about British and American responsibility for the allegedly shameful outrage inflicted upon Japan 20 years ago next Summer in the shape of the atom bomb.

Last year, if his memory served aright, this feeling was responsible for, amongst other things, the publicised planting of some Japanese flowering cherry trees in Ipswich with an accompanying inscription deploring the use of the bomb against two Japanese cities.

"Rather understandably, I thought, the cherry trees were found uprooted next morning," said the Canon.

If the bomb had not been dropped the resultant casualties would have been far higher than they were upon that day. The war in the Far East would have wound its weary way through carnage upon carnage, leaving marks in the minds of men and sears upon the face of the Japanese homeland that long would have remained to tell the tale. An intensified aerial offensive after the pattern of that used on Germany would have caused havoc with the Japanese civilian population in their crowded cities and with their totally inadequate civil defence.

"The Japanese soldiery would have fought like wild animals against the invaders landing on their shores," continued Canon Godfrey," and this much I can vouch for personally, as can many another East Anglian, that the moment the invader landed every one of the thousands of Allied prisoners in their hands was to have been shot or otherwise done to death.

"Great indeed was the slaughter and destruction at Hiroshima and Nagasaki, but greater far would have been the slaughter and destruction if the weapons of conventional warfare alone had been employed to bring that conflict to an end and that is one of the ironies of history."

He said they could not build up the Kingdom of God upon a lie. Evil things were done in wartime by all participants, all had trespasses for which they needed to be forgiven, all had need to forgive trespasses of others against themselves. But far better than planting provocative cherry trees was the action now being taken by the Church and people of Coventry in launching an appeal to provide a hospital for Dresden, another of the large-scale victims of the horror of modern war.

"The day could come when a joint big Anglo-American hospital could be set up in Hiroshima as a similar gesture, and what a gesture it could be."

'East Anglian Daily Times' (Extract)
9 November 1964

Ⓑ SIR—With memories of last year I kept careful watch on this year's Remembrance Sunday.

On an active North London high-road-cum-trunk-road there was almost no response to the first maroon, at 11 a.m., which was clearly heard. One teenager looked at his watch and walked on. A solitary car stopped and the driver stood beside it. A bus remained still for the full two minutes. The car driver could not stay the course and drove off just before the second maroon.

No pedestrian at all stood still. This is a very marked contrast with the situation in the years between the wars, when every vehicle and every walker remained immobile.

If any further proof were needed to demonstrate the total futility of our educational systems this is it.

This century has claimed nearly one hundred million martyrs. We have learned nothing whatever from their deaths. The world situation today proves this much too well. For many hundreds of years philosophers and historians have said not one word worth saying.

Immense sums of money are spent on schooling, but we remain as moronic, non-thinking, non-reflecting and non-adult as ever.

Yours truly,
PETER LONSDALE.
London, N.16.

Ⓒ Sir—Might I presume to write some form of defence of the "moronic generation" so bitterly condemned by your correspondent on Nov. 19 for its failure to keep the two-minute silence on Remembrance Sunday.

I was working on Remembrance Sunday, making beds in the home for elderly people in which I work. At 11 o'clock I heard the maroon. My memories of the war are limited to a much-hated Mickey Mouse gas-mask. I lost no beloved relative and suffered no real discomfort. Like other members of my generation the last war has taken a place in history.

Don't blame us that we were born too late. Please don't disparage us because we are not called upon to die for our country. There are many of us who in serving God are attempting to live for our country.

As I continued making the beds I thanked God for the lives of those who have in the past won freedom for us.

Remembrance is not enough. Dare I suggest that two minutes spent in a critical survey of those who are not standing to attention is not worthy of those you remember? Why not positive prayer and work for the future of mankind?

I did not hear the second maroon. I was still making beds.
Yours faithfully,
MARGARET BOYNES.
Clacton-on-Sea, Essex.

'The Daily Telegraph'
11 November 1964

Gas, Electricity & Landscape

ⒶGas burns brightly in Wales

by IAN NAIRN

'A real improvement.' The shop (above) that became Chepstow's gas showroom (below).

VISITORS to Wales do not need to be told that the average level of architecture there is pretty low: they will see soon enough for themselves.

The native designers, who did so well with the chapels and terraces almost up to 1900, never seem to have recovered from the grandiose stylistic exercises dumped on them from across the border through the years. In the last 60 years Welsh architects often seem to have had an inferiority complex about building something simple and have tried to out-do the invaders, usually in the style before last.

There are bright spots. One that an observant traveller might notice is in the showrooms of the Welsh Gas Board. They are always modern, always decent, never stereotyped—a refreshing change, this—and sometimes brilliant. For an example look at the before and after photographs of the new premises at Chepstow, next to the town gate, which is such a trial to the heavy lorries grinding up the steep main street. With the very simplest of materials — roof-slates, white-painted brickwork and black trim—the designers have created a real town improvement, a shop which gives a genuine lift to the street. It is also, incidentally, an extremely effective advertisement; compare it with the dowdy fussiness of Boots next door.

Tidy minded

The designers were Alex Gordon and Partners of Cardiff; they are architects to the Board, and Gordon himself has the status of a Chief Officer. The firm is integrated so closely that it sees and comments on every drawing for new installations. The engineers regard them simply as part of the team—"they have turned out," says Gordon a little ominously,

"to be more tidy minded than we are ourselves."

This is a remarkable example of industrial patronage, and it was initiated by a remarkable man, T. Mervyn Jones, who became chairman of the Board when it was started up in 1949. He was then the youngest board chairman in the country, and he is now the only one remaining of the original nominees.

His job was to modernise what seemed on the face of it to be a dying industry—who in 1950 would have prophesied more than a few more years of life for gas, as the messy stoves and hissing fires were slowly scrapped in favour of clean, new electricity? The appliances had to be modernised, of course, but so had the whole image of gas. "Changing the corporate image" is a technique used too often, and frequently without any real point—the brewers, in particular, seem to switch fashions every other week—but here it was essential. With 108 separate and antiquated plants and a tradition of showrooms decorated part-time by Jones the Gas, there was a lot of leeway to be made up.

The plants are now rationalised, the latest stage being a new £6,000,000 plant at Llandarcy, near Swansea. The showrooms are

almost entirely redesigned—except, oddly enough, the one in Cardiff itself—by Gordon the Drawing Board and his partners. One of them designed the Board's new headquarters in Cardiff, an elegant curtain-walled slab which is easily the best modern building in the city.

Wise words

To quote from one of the Board's own reports, "The Board has learnt much from this engineer-architect collaboration. Honest, courageous engineering has been seen to be the best and soundest architecture. Skilled architectural design has proved to be efficient and economical in engineering."

Wise words and a noble 17-year record of patronage. If the electricity people had followed the lead of gas and actually done something about their works — particularly small substations — instead of mounting a vast advertising campaign to convince the public that they couldn't, the face of Britain might not look quite so much of a mess.

'The Observer'
19 June 1969

Spoiling Britain

B SIR,—Ian Nairn is quite right when he contrasts the attitude of the Gas Board and the Electricity Board to the appearance of their installations.

Nearly eight years ago, to celebrate the opening of its North Wales grid, the Gas Board constructed a lay-by on the A5 road near Menai Bridge as a viewpoint for one of our finest landscapes. The Menai Strait lies in the foreground, Snowdonia is majestic in the distance, with green countryside in between, as a frame to the picture there are two fine bridges—Telford's Menai Suspension Bridge and Stephenson's Tubular Railway Bridge. Both are superb pieces of architecture and important examples of engineering history.

Of the Gas Grid itself nothing is visible; it is all underground. Now the Electricity Board is completing the nuclear power station at Wylfa Head in Anglesey, and the march of giant pylons is not only visible but makes a great scar across the flat landscape. The inland part of the island is not renowned for its beauty but the coast is, and at the crossing of the Menai Strait the pylons have been sited immediately behind the Tubular Bridge. They are so huge that although they stand on the shore their tops are clearly visible above the towers of the

bridge and the ugly cables make nonsense of its clean lines. Beyond, the pylons lead the eye to the mountains. This deliberate affront to our sensibilities is what you may now see if you stand at the Gas Board's viewpoint.

Why did the Electricity Board choose to destroy this beautiful view? If it was really too expensive or technically impossible to lay a short length of cable under the Strait it would have been simple to re-route it half a mile or so to the south, where it would have been out of sight from this point. The level of architecture in Wales is indeed low, as your contributor says, but much of the scenery is outstanding. If its despoliation continues at the present rate, there will soon be very little left for our visual enjoyment.

Charles L. Mowat, Professor of History.
Frank V. Thomas, Pianist, Department of Music.
J. Gwynn Williams, Professor of Welsh History.
Anthony D. Bradshaw, Reader in Agricultural Botany.
Maurice E. Cooke, Senior Lecturer in the History of Art.
Reginald Smith Brindle, Reader in Music.
University College of North Wales.

C Sir,—Ian Nairn in his article "Gas burns brightly in Wales" refers to lack of design by Electricity Boards of small sub-stations. In the British Isles these sub-stations number approximately 150,000 and are being built nationally at the rate of more than 6,000 per year.

If the present growth of the load doubling every seven years is maintained, then in 20 years' time there will be three times the present number of sub-stations. Is it really reasonable to expect these sub-stations to be individually designed?

We do not believe that the majority of people notice or condemn these so-called eye-sores of power stations, overhead lines or sub-stations. They are accepted by the majority as part of the pattern of modern living. Are they not a measure of this country's well-being and continually rising living standards?

Perhaps your correspondent would prefer electrical sub-stations to resemble Gas Board showrooms. Should we achieve this Utopian state, how does he suggest we disguise electrical pylons to resemble gasometers.

A. W. F. Hooper
Lindfield.   **D. G. Chugg**
'The Observer'
26 June 1966

D The trouble arises when the power they generate in these remote regions has to be moved to the users, which means all of us. However designed, a 165-foot pylon, which is needed to carry 4,000,000-volt lines, is bound to be obtrusive. These pylons have had the best designers money can buy, but they still obtrude.

I go at once halfway to CEGB's case in agreeing that one line of giant pylons is less offensive than a network of lesser power lines. What has been called the 'wirescape' is intolerable, and we have a great many examples of it in Kent.

There remains strong and unrelenting demands that in areas of outstanding beauty some of these 4,000,000-volt lines should go underground. A very strong plea was made for this on that section of the Dungeness line running between Bolney and Lovedean in Sussex.

The Generating Board's short answer is that it costs £366,000 to underground a mile of heavy-duty 275-kV. cable, which is 13 times as much as the cost of the overhead line. They add, with an eye on the farmers, that this needs two trenches, each 5 feet wide and at least 6 feet between them—with the prospect of disturbance if things go wrong.

For the Supergrid they can offer even more daunting figures. A mile of 4,000,000-volt cable put underground would cost £1,056,000 or 20 times as much as the equivalent overhead line. With the water cooling pipes which

would be necessary four trenches would be required, each 3 feet wide with at least 6 feet between them.

I am as suspicious of this argument as the next man; £1 million a mile is a powerful figure. It drowns argument. Between Bolney and Lovedean it would have involved some £40 million.

One has an unworthy suspicion that it would be a worrying day for the CEGB when someone offered to do the job very much cheaper. Meanwhile, it is fair to ask the question: who would pay? Is everyone to share an extra rental charge for these underground lines? Or should it be shared among those in the immediate environment?

Should the Government subsidise it and charge the taxpayer? And what of those who say: 'I don't mind the pylons; I refuse to pay my share of the underground cost'?

Much can be done by picking the right route—this occupied months on the Sussex side of Dungeness, and Miss Sylvia Crowe, a leading and enlightened landscape architect, was employed to give the best advice which is already available from Lord Holford, a part-time member of the Board.

Generally, skylines are avoided whenever possible. 'Advantage is taken of background'—I am quoting a recent publication of the CEGB—'and lines are routed so that, where practicable, their appearance is broken up by trees'.

There remain many places where the choice lies between destroying a valley or a crest and the Board cannot win.

They are bound to offend.

Where does this leave us? First, clearly, the need for unceasing public vigilance is established. It keeps the CEGB alert, anxious to please, to avoid displeasing. If we cease to care, why should they?

Secondly, I think there is room for wider appreciation of the grandeur of power. We judge emanations of the CEGB not on their merits, which aesthetically and by contrast with a lot of unsightly rubbish being built (on farms as well as in towns) are high, but as just one more blot on the rural landscape.

This is a natural reaction. Is it a true appreciation? I think those who tell us we shall—or must—grow accustomed to the noise of giant jets—need their heads examining. I am not convinced that they are wrong who tell us that we shall come to assimilate and accept pylons, as we have railways.

Finally, we should examine critically the state of mind these protests against power stations and power lines betray. It is a split frame of mind. On one hand, we speak of the need to modernise this country, to equip her for the 21st century. In the same breath we declare that the passage of electric power is rendering the country unfit to live in. As motorists we declare that the roads programme is pitiful, and as dwellers in the countryside that motorways are ruinous.

'Kent Messenger'
3 September 1966

Pylons Threat to Constable Country "Not Local Issue"

NATIONAL TRUST OPPOSITION

E Valley Held For Benefit of Nation

Fears that the picturesque "Constable" countryside in the Stour Valley would be "mutilated" by pylons and overhead power lines, were expressed yesterday at the second day's hearing of the Brantham public inquiry on the Central Electricity Generating Board's proposals to run an overhead line from Brantham to Lawford for the purpose of improving supplies in the Colchester area.

Mr. N. de Bazille Corbin, Eastern area agent for the National Trust, said the Stour Valley was of outstanding scenic importance, and was held by the Trust for the benefit of the nation.

He pointed out that Flatford Mill, the Mill House and Willy Lott's cottage, together with 16 acres of land, had been bought by the Trust in 1943, and that since 1946 the Field Studies Council had been tenants.

The Council, which was closely associated with universities and many scientific bodies, held study courses over the countryside.

More than 100 artists, who came to Flatford because of its charm and beauty, had spent periods in residence there since May.

"STEEL HORRORS"

Flatford's associations with John Constable made it virtually a national shrine.

He concluded: "This is one of our most important properties. We were entrusted with it because of its national importance, and we have statutory obligations to protect and preserve the setting.

"If the Board's scheme takes place it will be a catastrophe," he said.

Another objector, Mr. Ralph Dreschfield, secretary of the Essex branch of the Council for Preservation for Rural England, deplored the "steel horrors" and suggested the Board should be honest and say, "We propose to ruin the countryside, and this is the cheapest way to do it."

Mr. Frederick Westropp, secretary of the Suffolk Preservation Society, said "I ask that we should not have to suffer the conglomeration of wires across the fields."

Brigadier Sidney Collingwood, secretary of the Dedham Vale Preservation Society, said the popularity of the beauty spots had increased considerably during the past 12 years, and between 30,000 and 40,000 people visited Flatford Mill during the Summer season.

On special days, he said, traffic was so heavy that special constables were called out on duty to assist the police.

Brigadier Collingwood said he regarded the threat of pylons as a national issue because visitors came to Flatford from all parts of the country and from all parts of the world.

Mr. Leslie Fisher, deputy County Planning Adviser for Essex County Council, said it appeared that the Board might well be under-estimating the future demand in the Colchester area, having regard to the increase of population in the forthcoming years.

A figure of 100,000 had already been estimated and a decision had now been taken to establish a University of Essex, which may increase this figure significantly.

AN ALTERNATIVE

Urging that the Constable country should not be despoiled, he said that the part of North-East Essex between Harwich and Dedham was of great value, both scenically and historically.

There were already overhead power lines between Dedham and Lawford village which were ugly to look at, and the addition of any more would be detrimental to the landscape.

Referring to the investigations being carried out for the siting of a new power station near Harwich he said that if the proposal proceeded it was the Board's intention that the station should be operating by about 1970, and that power would need to be conveyed by a line from Harwich to a proposed new switchgear station South of Braintree.

This station was also being designed to receive a new power line from North Essex, where it would be connected into the new power line from Sizewell nuclear power station.

He added: "If the Harwich power station is built the line from there to Braintree would need to pass through the heart of the Colchester area. If this would serve the future power demands which are estimated for 1969 it would save the Stour Valley from spoiliation by overhead power lines."

UNDERGROUND CABLES

Mr. R. M. Beechey, for East Suffolk County Council, said the Council joined with Essex County Council in asking whether the Board had looked far enough ahead in its overall planning of lines in the area.

As regards the extra costs for underground cables, he submitted that this was "a drop in the ocean," and spread over a long period would be a small sum to ask.

It was certainly not too much of a price to pay to preserve a landscape area of great value.

Mr. Thomas Oxenbury, East Suffolk County Planning Officer, said with the exception of the Brantham industrial area the Stour Valley and Dedham Vale were valuable landscape areas.

The industrial works had been on this site, however, for many years, and the County Council had to accept the works in this position as "a legacy of the past."

He said: "My Council feel strongly that this area, which is already crossed by existing electricity lines, should not be further spoiled by another major electricity line, even though it will now be sited to follow the railway. It is felt it would still be an intrusion into the appearance of this area."

Recalling that the Minister had urged on local authorities the necessity of protecting the coastal areas, which also included major estuaries, he said: "The Stour can be regarded as a major estuary, and every effort should be made to preserve and improve its appearance."

'East Anglian Daily Times'
25 October 1963

Pylons not according to Bronte, inquiry told

(F) The National Parks Commission objected strongly at the public inquiry at Keighley yesterday to any proposal to erect electricity pylons in the Brontë country, where " the whole setting, the colour, the great sweep of dark moorland, the scale of the place, is true to all that one pictures from the Brontë books."

Mrs Pauline Dower, giving evidence for the commission, said that the sheer size of the electricity pylons—they would be about 165ft. high—would dwarf everything else and be a strongly discordant element across the landscape. She added:

"Trying to reconstruct for oneself the 'feel' of the Brontë country would become almost impossible with so flagrant and omnipresent an intrusion cutting across a view."

Yesterday was the fifth day of the inquiry into the Central Electricity Generating Board's application for a 400kV. line up carry Yorkshire's surplus electricity across the Pennines from Bradford to Darwen. The choice of three routes is at stake: the so-called " red " route (which the Generating Board favours), which runs south of the Brontë village of Haworth; the " blue " route, across Wadsworth Moor; and the " green " route, which runs near the built-up areas of Brighouse, Elland, and Ripponden.

Incalculable value

Mr J. G. H. Mackrell, representing a group of objectors in the Haworth area, referred Mrs Dower to her evidence that the moorland was of incalculable value, and asked : " Of more value than the £1 million bandied about at this inquiry ? " (The extra cost of the " green " route has been put at about £1 million.) Mrs Dower replied : " Certainly of incalculable value. It is a very big tourist draw."

Mr David Tattersall, a senior assistant planning officer with Lancashire County Council, said the " red " route would pass close to Wycoller, a hamlet with Brontë associations, before crossing the watershed by the Herders Road.

The inquiry continues today.

'The Guardian'
6 July 1966

(G) The public inquiry into the proposed Yorkshire-Lancashire power line was told before it closed yesterday that if the admiration of past writers was unhealthy, " then our wonderful heritage of English literature is doomed."

This reply to an earlier reference to " an unhealthy worship of the Brontës " was made by Mr Albert Preston, a member of the council of the Brontë Society. He criticised the " red " route— one of the three alternatives proposed—which would take the pylons south of the Brontës' home village of Haworth.

" To the thousands who have read and still read the Brontë novels the spirit of the local moors has so impressed itself that it would be a sad day for all if these moors were to be desecrated by a line of high pylons and thick cables. However carefully planned, the pylons would destroy for ever the sense of grandeur, solitude, and barrenness which inspired the creation of those characters which have made such an impact on the world,"

Mr T. B. Sutcliffe, secretary of the Hardcastle Crags Preservation Society, opposed the " blue " route which runs across Wadsworth Moor. He felt the " red " would not be so detrimental. He added :

" Although it is representative of the West Riding, the landscape of the ' red ' route is not as beautiful as the Hardcastle Crags area which is largely unique. Further, people do not visit that area for its scenic beauty as is the case of Hardcastle Crags, but for its literary associations."

After the hearing, the inspectors adjourned to inspect the three suggested routes which the Central Electricity Generating Board hopes to use for the 400,000-volt overhead line from Bradford to Darwen.

'The Guardian'
7 July 1966

Warnings to Children

A There was once a naughty little girl, who did not care for what her mamma said to her; and one morning, though she had been told not to go into the street by herself, she set off the very first time she saw the door open. She was so silly as to fancy she could take care of herself, and find her way back again as soon as she wished to go home; so she went along, first into one street, and then into another, looking about at all the things that she passed, and never once thinking about home; she never thought how unhappy her mamma would be, when she found that her little girl was gone from home. At last she began to feel tired, and thought she would go home again; but, when she turned round, she could not tell which way to go; she walked about through one street after another, but could not see any house that looked like her mamma's.

After she had been out a long time, she began to feel very hungry; and, when she looked at the shops which had nice cakes at their windows, she wished very much for some of them. She had no money, nor anybody with her to buy her some of them. The longer she walked, the farther she was from home; for she had got into places that she had never seen before; and she began to feel very much afraid.

At length, she saw that night was coming on, and that it would very soon be dark. She was besides tired, and cold, and hungry, and she began to cry sadly. She thought what a sad thing it would be to stay in the street all the night, without any bed to sleep on, or anything to keep her warm; she wished very much that she had not been such a naughty girl, but had minded what her mamma had said to her. She found that the people, who passed her in the street, were not so kind and good as her mamma; they did not seem to care about her, though she cried very loud, and was shivering with cold.

It grew so dark that she could not see the people near her; but a woman closely passing her, saw her, and asked her what was the matter; the little girl told her that she had lost herself, and could not find the way back to her mamma's house. The woman said she would take her to it; and the little girl was very glad; and, after they had walked a long way, they came to a house, but the little girl knew it was not her mamma's. She said: 'This is not my mamma's house; my mamma's house has steps to go up to the door, and a lamp at the top, which always burns at night'. The woman said, 'I know very well this is not your mamma's house; it is mine, and you are my little girl now'.

The little girl cried very much, and begged to be taken home; but the woman said, 'No, you will never see home again, nor your mamma, nor your brothers, nor sisters; for I shall keep you, and I shall beat you if you tell any one this is not your home'. The little girl cried more than before, but she did not dare to say a word, for the naughty woman showed her the large whip, which, she said, she would beat her with, if she spoke. Then she took off the clothes the little girl had on, and put her on some old shabby ones, and took her into a ship, which was near the house. Very soon after the ship sailed away, and this naughty little girl never saw her kind mamma or her nice home, any more.

From 'Pleasing and Instructive Stories for Young Children', by Mary Hughes (London, Wm. Darton, 1821).

A COMIC FROM YOUR POLICEMAN

READ IT AND ASK YOUR PARENTS ABOUT IT

FOR CHILDREN

The **Cautious Twins**

Doreen and Dan, the Cautious Twins, live in our neighbourhood. They ask their Mother where to play as all good children should.

If someone in a motor car should offer you a ride, Shout loudly "No!" and run away, but do not get inside.

If you can read the NUMBER plate, repeat it in your mind, Or write it down upon the ground with anything you find.

If someone that you do not know should offer you a treat; Remember how he looks and talks. but run fast up the street.

If someone tells you he was sent to take you home to Dad, Run, tell the teacher or police, perhaps that man is bad.

A person may invite you to a house, garage or shed, Say "No!" to him and run and tell your mother what he said.

It's wonderful to play with friends at playgrounds or a park, But cautious kids all hurry home before they find it's dark.

THE DEATH OF A FATHER

Oh, fatal stroke!—must hope expire,
  And shall my tender parent die?
The ghastly monarch, with charg'd quiver
  Points his poniard—mocks my cry.

Father, does his arrows pierce thee?
  Reclines thy heart against its wall;
Faint and trembling art thou sinking,
  Tastes thy lips the bitter'd gall?

Does thy weaken'd fabric tremble—
  Will the grave my parent hide?
Oh! The stroke—I cannot bear it,
  Must I lose my tenderest guide.

Father! tell me, art thou dying?
  Lingers yet thy quivering breath:
Is the foe the conquest gaining,
  Must thou yield to conqu'ring death?

Thy eye-balls sinking in their sockets,
  Closing, shut to ope' no more:
Thy spirit quits its falling temple,
  Quits to seek another shore.

This hour robs me of my father,
  New-born troubles rise to birth:
Fatherless, and unprotected,
  Cold he sinks to mother earth.

Floods of tears, could you relieve me,
  Surely I'd relief obtain;
But, oh! my breaking heart assures me,
  You can't assuage—tears flow in vain.

Chill'd is my prospect—let me linger
  Let me wash thy sacred bier
With those tears I would deposit
  In the grave with thee, dear sire.

Greedy grave—respite thy victim,
  Suspend thy yawnings while I weep;
Take thy little infant mourner,
  Let me with my father sleep.

Oh, the sexton's delving weapon
  Shows no pity to a child;
Thy steel is polished with the ashes
  Of death's victims—Oh, I'm wild!

O, how cruel! death has seiz'd him,
  And the grave's cold bosom yawns
To receive her cold deposit,
  Chills my hopes and sinks as dawns.

Heaven pardon, if I murmur,
  'Tis a child whose father's dead;
And the turf now hides its parent,
  All its hopes are with him fled.

Children, prize a tender father,
  Best protectors of the young;
Never let your conduct grieve them,
  Never vex them with your tongue.

'The Guardian'
10 June 1966

BLACKMAILED INTO VIRTUE

by Margaret Rickards

"**E**VERY intelligent parent," says the "Affectionate Parent's Gift and Good Child's Reward," "will acknowledge the existing difficulty in making a suitable selection of subjects to attract the attention of Juvenile Readers, and in clothing the sentiments intended to be conveyed to infant minds in language suitable to their capacities of comprehension."

The aim of making children's books good for, attractive to, and easily read by them seems admirably enlightened for 1828, the year in which this volume was published, but a modern parent might be startled by the author's methods of achieving it. Did the good children whose reward it became really enjoy it? Almost all the book's poems and essays fall into three categories: nature, and the morals to be drawn from observing it; charity towards the poor; and death. These are varied by the occasional description of a family outing—

"Come, child, with me, a father said,
I often have a visit paid
To yon receptacle of woe
For Lunatics. Come, child, and know."

Crusts and solitary confinement

A particularly detailed description of one of the inmates of the "receptacle," chained to the ground, screeching and tearing his hair, is accompanied by an illustration of the infant being held up by Daddy, as at the zoo, to peer through the grating. Its expression is serene and placid. Other visits were organised by affectionate fathers, notably—

"A walk through Newgate with the lads
Just for example's sake."

Here they saw what happened to small sinners, in solitary confinement with crusts and water.

The deaths of both parents are celebrated, in a horribly prolonged manner, in the course of the book; both are pictured reclining quietly in frilled nightcaps, arms arranged neatly above the sheets, surrounded by weeping children. In one picture, a child wards off a threatening skeleton armed with a lethal dart. (Decorum survives death—the skeleton is carefully draped where modesty requires.)

"Oh fatal stroke!—must hope expire
And shall my tender parent die?
The ghastly monarch, with charg'd quiver
Points his poniard—mocks my cry."

The intention here, apparently, was to persuade the child to appreciate his father before it was too late.

The attention of the upper-class readers is frequently diverted to the poor and afflicted—the blind fiddler, the orphans selling gingerbread or matches, the child sweep whose mother was reduced to selling *him*. Since the declared object of the book, however, was to promote the reader's "temporal Prosperity and eternal Happiness," in that order, the afflicted seldom received more than a token coin from the child heroines of the stories, who then returned to their comfortable homes feeling disproportionately smug—

"I never in my life have felt
More sweetly satisfied,"

says Mary to her sister, who has not been quite so generous.

The "contemplative Child" was invited to study Nature, but for the morals it supplied rather than for its own sake. The docile Cow, the uncomplaining Horse, the industrious Bee, all aided the parents' cause in providing models for the young. That was before the days of nature red in tooth and claw. There were plenty of storms, shipwrecks, and volcanoes to impress on the children the consequences of supernatural wrath—

"The gaping earth its prey devours,
Its victims in its chasms pours"—
illustrated by bodies crushed under falling wreckage. "Tremble, oh child, to sin!"; the day of judgment will be worse than this.

The worst sin of all

In this Old Testament framework, gratitude is urged unceasingly on the child; because his parents are still alive to take him on visits to Newgate, because he is not blind, mad, or actively ill-treated, or because he has not been born a pig instead of a human being. And the worst sin of all is to disobey the fifth commandment. It has a whole poem to itself, and holds out dire threats.

"Then where's the child who dare oppose
The Sovereign Laws of heaven,
Who dare his parents disobey
And hope to be forgiven."

It all sounds like a plot to grind the parental axe and keep the good child under, the naughty ones having been disposed of by Newgate and hellfire. Were the good ones successfully blackmailed into virtue and subservience? Did any suspicion cross their minds, reading the undisguised moral at the end of every story, that they were being got at? This was the upbringing which produced the adults of the Victorian upper classes, comfortable in the knowledge that their own temporal prosperity and eternal happiness were assured.

Probably parents and children alike believed in its effectiveness as sincerely as the modern parent believes in Spock. It did give the children the security of a consistent view of life and code of conduct imposed from above, and if their introduction to the idea of death was unnecessarily horrific, at least the issue was not evaded. Our children, persuaded in the way that they should go by love and psychology rather than fear and enforced gratitude, are more fortunate. Only the future can tell us whether they will turn out more virtuous.

'The Guardian'
10 June 1966

Marrying Young

John Grigg

Young marriage

(A) AMERICANS HAVE LONG been in the habit of marrying (for the first time) young, and the habit has now spread to Britain. Although marriage under the age of 21 still requires the consent of parents or of a magistrates' court, the number of minors getting married in Britain has been increasing dramatically.

The total number of bridegrooms under 21 increased from 45,000 in 1962 to 52,000 in 1964 (14 per cent of all males who were married in that year), while the figure for brides went up from 136,000 to 146,000 (41 per cent of all women married in 1964). It is probable that almost half of all the girls now being married in Britain are under 21.

A high proportion of the marriages are of the "shot-gun" variety. In 1964 nearly 18,000 girls of 16 and 17 were married in England and Wales, of whom nearly 11,000 gave birth to children within seven months of marriage.

The impact of youthful marriage upon the divorce figures has been predictably heavy. In 1963, of a total of roughly 32,000 dissolutions and annulments in England and Wales, about 10,000 wives and 1,700 husbands involved had been under 20 at the time of marriage—i.e. about a third of the total. And one should add that nearly all the remainder were married in the age-group 20-24.

Some idea of the number of children now being afflicted with broken homes can be obtained by comparing the divorce with the birth-rate figures. Legitimate births to mothers under 21 increased from 88,000 in 1962 to 99,000 in 1964, and for fathers under 21 the figures were 25,000 and 31,000 respectively.

American doubts

UNTIL RECENTLY, the United States was peculiar among advanced countries in the tendency of its people to marry young. Only in Asia was there a comparable marriage pattern, but now Britain at any rate is going the same way.

In America, more girls marry at 18 than at any other age, and it has been estimated that half of all young men are married before they are 25. Moreover, the average mother has her last child at the age of 26.

The social pressure on young Americans to get married is overwhelming. Little or no stigma attaches to being divorced, but unmarried men in their thirties and unmarried women in their late twenties are likely to be objects of pity or contempt.

There is evidence that Americans are beginning to worry about the demographic, if not the social and moral, effects of early marriage. A professor of law, Professor Albert P. Blaustein, made a statement on March 2 to a Senate subcommittee in which he argued that "one of the best ways to help limit the population explosion is to encourage delays in marriage," and even suggested, among other things, that preference might be given to single persons applying for scholarships.

One would guess, however, that legal and institutional restraints will be of little avail

41

unless and until the social atmosphere changes. So long as young people feel impelled to marry early, their elders will not make matters significantly better, and may even make matters worse, by trying to rig the rules against them.

False maturity

WHAT ARE THE REASONS for rushing into marriage? One all too frequent reason, as the figures show, is that a child has been conceived. Yet in such cases, the parents, far from loving each other in any real sense, may be little more than casual acquaintances. Marriages which occur as an alternative to abortion or illegitimacy are unlikely to be happy and will often come unstuck.

But even without the duress of a pregnancy, the urge to get married in extreme youth is evidently growing, and it may well be connected with the desire to demonstrate maturity. Since marriage is traditionally regarded as a state at which people arrive when they are mature, it may easily be thought that maturity can be achieved simply by getting married.

Granted that there are exceptions to any rule, it would seem that the disadvantages of early marriage hugely outweigh the advantages. For the partners themselves there is the obvious danger that what they take to be love is, in fact, only calf-love, and there is anyway a lot of sense in the old-fashioned doctrine that before taking on the responsibilities of home and family one should first be established in life.

For women, the arguments against early marriage are even stronger than for men. If the teenage girls now caught up in the matrimonial stampede feel that they are asserting their liberty, they could hardly be more mistaken, because they are actually denying themselves much of the benefit of female emancipation. It was understandable that women should marry young when their only function was to bear children and act as household drudges, but now that an ever-widening range of work is open to them their obsession with marriage is a most strange paradox.

But of course the chief victims of premature marriage are the children. Young couples would surely be less impulsive and carefree if they could visualise the effects of what they do and decide upon the next generation.

'The Guardian'
12 May 1966

Mariage a la Mods

Ⓑ Sir,—Surely John Grigg, in his article of May 12, overlooks the most frequent reason for young marriages—namely, the tendency to start courtship early. In America, and increasingly in this country as well, adolescents begin "dating" at 13 or 14. From here, the next stage is that of "going steady," and this, because of the prestige and security it confers within their own age-group, is often reached by the age of 16 or earlier.

It becomes almost inevitable, then, that such a relationship should lead to marriage, since few teenagers—especially girls—possess the stability and self-reliance to contemplate the break-up of what has by now become a very close partnership. They are surprised how rapidly the habit of another person's company is formed, especially if the two concerned are sleeping together as well as seeing one another almost daily. They leap to the conclusion that this must be "real love." Thus they marry, at the age of 18 or 19, since the wedding day seems the logical and only culmination to the years of "going steady," and few have clearly envisaged the 50 or 60 years of marriage that may lie beyond.

The remedy, surely, is to try to reverse the fashion which decrees that a "steady" at 16 or 17 is a status-symbol, and educate teenagers for the often grim and disillusioning realities of marriage which follow that romantic walk in the spotlight to the altar.—Yours etc.,

(Mrs) **A. M. Lambert.**

London, N.6

'The Guardian'
14 May 1966

Youth at the altar

Ⓒ Sir,—As a newly-wed father-to-be of 20, I feel that John Grigg's article on young marriages (May 12) merits a reply.

Divorce does not result from young marriages, but from the defects in our social system, of which the tendency to marry younger is but a symptom. Personally I am fed up with influential voices from the mass media continually telling my wife and me that we can look forward to bitterness and disillusionment in the divorce court fighting over the driftwood of our wrecked lives; that is, our children.

I fully agree that some young marriages have little hope of success because one or both of the partners are too immature. But if everybody waited for complete maturity before their nuptials most of us would be gliding gracefully down the aisle in wheel chairs.—Yours faithfully,
David R. G. Weeks.

Newcastle upon Tyne

'The Guardian'
17 May 1966

Ⓓ

DO YOU think that people should be allowed to marry before the age of 21 without either their parents or a court giving permission?

That notoriously staid body, the British Medical Association, thinks that boys and girls are old enough to assume full responsibility for the decision at 18.

In the evidence they submitted to the Committee on the Age of Majority they said that "from the medical point of view there appears to be no reason why the age at which young people may marry without parental consent should not be lower than 21."

I find this confusing. Surely the building of a marriage and the upbringing of children does not depend on the simple fact that a couple is old enough to conceive?

This seems to me to reduce human beings to the status of animals.

Other people agree with the B M A and have said so to this Committee of Inquiry set up by the Lord Chancellor, Lord Gardiner, last summer to consider whether changes are desirable in the law affecting the rights of minors.

The right to marry, to vote, to drive, to drink, to smoke, to buy a house, raise money or place a bet.

The Free Church Federal Council (although not altogether certain among themselves) have also suggested that the age for marriage-without-consent be lowered to 18. But that the age of sexual consent be raised from 16 to 18.

They, too, mention earlier physical maturing, and add that by the age of 18 young people "often earn high wages and it seems they should accept corresponding responsibilities."

Their third point is that "as young people

ANNE ALLEN

The writer who gets to the heart of things

Is eighteen too young to marry without consent?

are quite likely to be out of home influence and parental care long before 21, it is unreasonable to expect parents to be responsible for them."

Wage

▓ I AM NOW floundering badly. Because I would not put the capacity to earn a good wage high on the list of marriage attributes when the people concerned may be babies emotionally.

I also happen to feel that it is perfectly reasonable to expect parents to take some responsibility for an unmarried child of nineteen or twenty.

Am I being excessively naive to want someone to mention maturity rather than age?

After all, in a recent survey THREE-QUARTERS of the young wives interviewed said that given another chance, they would never have married so young.

The National Marriage Guidance Council, too, is divided about the wisdom of early marriage.

They asked their counsellors whether the minimum age should be raised: 205 said "yes," 146 said "no." Three thought it should be *lowered*.

'Sunday Mirror'
29 May 1966

Genesis

Ⓐ

"Who are you?" said the Prime Minister, opening the door.

"I am God," replied the stranger.

"I don't believe you," sneered the Prime Minister. "Show me a miracle."

And God showed the Prime Minister the miracle of birth.

"Pah," said the Prime Minister. "My scientists are creating life in test-tubes and have nearly solved the secret of heredity. Artificial insemination is more certain than your lackadaisical method, and by cross-breeding we are producing fish and mammals to our design. Show me a proper miracle."

And God caused the sky to darken and hailstones came pouring down.

"That's nothing," said the Prime Minister, picking up the telephone to the Air Ministry. "Send up a met. plane would you, old chap, and sprinkle the clouds with silver chloride crystals."

And the met. plane went up and sprinkled the clouds which had darkened the world and the hailstones stopped pouring down and the sun shone brightly.

"Show me another," said the Prime Minister.

And God caused a plague of frogs to descend upon the land.

The Prime Minister picked up his telephone. "Get the Min. of Ag. and Fish," he said to the operator, "and instruct them to procure a frog-killer as myxomatosis killed rabbits."

And soon the land was free of frogs, and the people gave thanks to the Prime Minister and erected laboratories in his name.

"Show me another," sneered the Prime Minister.

And God caused the sea to divide.

The Prime Minister picked up his direct-link-telephone to the Polaris submarine.

"Lob a few ICBMs into Antarctica and melt the ice-cap, please, old man."

And the ice-cap melted into water and the sea came rushing back.

"I will kill all the first-born," said God.

"Paltry tricks," said the Prime Minister. "Watch this." He pressed a button on his desk.

And missiles flew to their pre-ordained destinations and H-bombs split the world asunder and radio-activity killed every mortal thing.

"I can raise the dead," said God.

"Please," said the Prime Minister in his cardboard coffin. "Let me live again."

"Why, who are you?" said God, closing the lid.

Brian Morris
'Weekend Telegraph'
29 October 1965

(B) Sir—I have never heard of Mr. Brian Morris, but his "Genesis" article in *Weekend Telegraph* is, to me, the perfect answer-in-a-nutshell to all the crazy outpourings of our modern atheistic age. It is both profound and succinct, with both humour and tragedy.

May we hear more from Mr. Morris, please, and congratulations on *Weekend Telegraph*.
Yours faithfully,
(Mrs.) VALERIE A. ELLISTON.
Hundon, Suffolk.

Blasphemy
(C) Sir—As a regular reader of your newspaper I was profoundly shocked by the "Genesis" article in *Weekend Telegraph*. This article constitutes, in my opinion, statements amounting to blasphemy in the eyes of the many decent readers of your paper. I have been led to expect from *The Daily Telegraph* something better than this, and I trust that such an article will never again take up a portion of your excellent colour magazine.

It is with great reluctance that I write this letter, but I feel that many others will resent this blatant affront to their so dearly-held convictions and that someone should speak up about this blight on your fine record.
Yours sincerely,
Glasgow.   ALAN J. GAMBLE.

'The Daily Telegraph'
6 November 1965

(D) Sir—I cannot understand Mr. Alan J. Gamble's statement in the letter published on Nov. 6 that the *Weekend Telegraph* article "Genesis" by Brian Morris amounted to blasphemy.

I thought it a brilliant piece of modern journalism, ironical and with a moral value, so shocking and true in its ending that I fail to see how anyone could be offended by the tone of reality in the article.

I would add that I am a practising Roman Catholic. I feel sure we will hear more of Mr. Morris in the future. Congratulations on your enterprise in publishing this article.   Yours faithfully,
PATRICK ALLEYN.
St. Paul's Cray, Kent.

'The Daily Telegraph'
13 November 1965

The New Morality

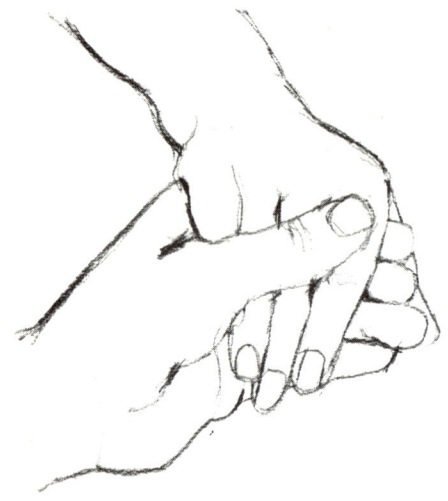

ELIMINATION OF JOY

"New Morality" Outlook on Chastity

(A) *From Sir CYRIL BLACK, M.P.*

Sir—What is the BBC up to? In a programme on Sunday evening, July 14, entitled "Sex and Family Life," a medical biologist said among other things:

A chivalrous boy is one who takes contraceptives with him when he goes to meet his girl friend.

Sex education should include instruction to the young on the intelligent and, correct use of foolproof contraceptives.

We might as well make up our minds that chastity is no more a virtue than malnutrition.

There is no reason why a man shouldn't have a mistress as well as a wife provided he is loyal to both.

And he gave two new Commandments to teenagers:

Thou shalt not under any circumstances produce an unwanted baby.

Thou shalt not exploit another's feelings.

At a time when the nation is gravely concerned at lowered moral standards what possible contribution to national well-being can such a programme make? When we remember the noble purposes and lofty idealism that John Reith brought to the BBC in its early days one can only deplore the calibre and standards of the people who at present mismanage its programmes.

Yours faithfully,
CYRIL BLACK.
House of Commons.

'The Daily Telegraph'
19 July 1963

(B) SIR—The intellectuals are indeed out of touch with facts, particularly the fact of Christian joy.

Dr. Comfort regards chastity as no more a virtue than malnutrition; indeed, according to his doctrine it is a form of malnutrition. Christians regard materialism as a form of malnutrition. A necessary food for the human soul is the joy in the love of God that comes from obedience to His laws.

The gradual elimination of this joy is evident everywhere: in our music, our art, our entertainment and our rising tide of crime.

Yours faithfully,
M. O. GOODMAN.
Orpington, Kent.

(C) Sir—Sir Cyril Black, M.P., in his otherwise excellent and timely letter on the "new morality" makes one mistake. He states that "the nation is gravely concerned at lowered moral standards."

Alas, the nation could not care less—only a minority is concerned.

Yours faithfully,
JAMES T. BRADLEY.
Croydon Elim Church, Surrey.

(D) Sir—Sir Cyril Black, M.P., deplored a recent BBC television programme "Sex and Family Life" on July 14. And the Rev. S. W. G. Elvins, a chaplain to a mother and baby home, also criticised Dr. Alex Comfort's two new Commandments, in the programme, on the premise that intellectual moralists are out of touch with the facts.

As a mother who listened to Dr. Comfort's excellent, commonsense talk I heartily disagree. As a programme I thought it was firstrate, and fully maintained the BBC's high standard of interest and educational value. With regard to Dr. Comfort's new Commandments —"Thou shalt not under any circumstances produce an unwanted baby" and "Thou shalt not exploit another's feelings"—surely nothing could be more Christian than these.

Far from being out of touch with the facts, they would seem to show that Dr. Comfort is obviously very much *in* touch with the facts. Here are clear rules, easily understood by all, which invest sex with its rightful sense of responsibility and which, if obeyed by teenagers and adults alike, would prevent the heartbreak and tragedy of unmarried mothers and unwanted children.
Yours faithfully,
CORINNE WHITTALL.
London, S.W.10.

(E) Sir—The "new morality" looks remarkably like the old immorality.

Yours faithfully,
Guildford.   M. J. DOUGLASS.

'The Daily Telegraph'
22 July 1963

(F) Dr. Comfort is not as bold as he would have us think. In his commandments he is actually hiding under the umbrella of the Christian ethic. Let him come out into the open and say what he means.

His commandments would seem to be really these: "Thou shalt not go out with the intention of indulging thy sexual appetite without taking contraceptives with you," and "Thou shalt not have intercourse with other persons without their willing co-operation." One could then admire him for his honesty if for nothing else.

Meanwhile let us continue to practise Christian love and self-discipline as the only secure basis for society, and treat with loving care those who fail to achieve this standard.   Yours faithfully,
JOHN S. LOXTON.
Burton-on-Trent.

'The Daily Telegraph'
24 July 1963

Two Sorts of Colour Problem

NEGRO IN MY LIFE

by Jennifer Rogers

WHEN I was at university I had a coloured boy friend. He was a very black Nigerian. I had always thought myself liberal and unprejudiced, but there's nothing like a bit of real, personal integration to make one realise, emotionally and intellectually, the problems of race relations.

From the first his charm, good looks, and integrity attracted me. But I freely admit that for the first few weeks I went out with him to see whether I could—as an act of defiance to myself. I felt self-conscious, defiant, and rather pleased with myself.

As far as I knew, my parents had never met a Negro in their lives. They are not narrow, intolerant, or bigoted, but I knew that they would regard marriage to a Negro by their daughter as involving them in obscure social disgrace. They knew nothing about this serious new friendship. When I had known him five months I arranged a meeting on neutral ground, introducing him very casually, but it was all pretty dismal. They were polite, faintly patronising, and talked in slow, careful, loud English. The prospect of telling them the truth was too painful, so I didn't and never have. Later I realised that this first deceit was really the first indication that I simply didn't have the courage a mixed marriage takes.

Our public appearances were greeted with indifference in university cities and the only

place our partnership regularly provoked more than simple curiosity was London. Possibly it was naïve of us to hold hands in Notting Hill, but we only needed to visit friends there to hear shouts from assorted yobs of " Go and —— your own kind ! " and other uninventive insults.

Gradually we acquired a freak novelty value in university society and were often invited to dinner by people who would never have bothered with us individually. We were always unofficial guests of honour on such occasions, the hostess invariably introducing us with a " Look what I've caught " sort of air. These dinner parties were usually embarrassing because of the clumsy tact with which any topic remotely connected with race was considered unmentionable.

These occasions were all the more intolerable to me because I recognised myself in them. The people who embarrassed us were only behaving as I would have behaved a few months earlier. The difficulty is that an English girl who has a Negro boy friend has to reconcile two standards, her own and his.

He was highly educated, more intelligent than me, his father was about ten times richer and more powerful than mine could ever hope to be. But it still irritated me that he held his knife like a pen, that he admired Hollywood he-men, and that he

wanted to carry those universal symbols of emancipated Africa, the umbrella and briefcase. I didn't like his immense collection of pop records eked out with the odd low-brow classic. I didn't like his father's promise of a huge American car the minute he returned home. I blamed these things quite consciously on the fact of his Negro race. I

was afraid other English people would criticise him for these things, so I criticised him instead, I tried to turn him, through my criticism, into an English gentleman and intellectual. Naturally, I failed. His gentle stubbornness was too much for me.

This failure didn't cure me of folly, as I then tried to turn myself into a Nigerian lady. It didn't actually go as far as boot polish on my face, but I did eat hot curries until my mascara ran, and I did, privately, practise wearing a wrappa—a Nigerian sari—which had an undignified way of falling off. I did learn to count in his language, but West African languages are difficult for Europeans and I am no linguist.

The crunch came when his brother wanted to marry an English girl. His father, mother, uncles, cousins, all wrote by turns angry, imploring letters pleading with him not to do such a ruinous thing. His career, his father's career and happiness, future generations . did he not see that all these would be jeopardised by marrying an English girl (i.e.

beneath him)? It was all so horrifyingly recognisable as what my own family would have said and done, but because it was the other way round it stung.

We quarelled quite a lot after this, so it wasn't as painful as it might have been when he went back to Nigeria. I never did fill in my application forms for a job there, but started my first job in England in the accustomed way.

Letters were frequent at first, but soon became more distant in tone. About two years later we were each safely married to someone of our own race and nationality. We sent each other pictures of the weddings, together with polite invitations—"Do come and see us if you're ever in our part of the world . . ."

'The Guardian'
18 May 1966

White girl in my life...

Ⓑ

THE article " Negro in my life," (May 18) prompted me to submit this little account of an episode in my life:

I met my English girl friend in Ceylon where she had come on a scholarship to do a year's postgraduate work at the university. At our very first meeting we realised that a strong physical attraction drew us to each other. I soon discovered that she also had a fine mind and a delightful sense of humour. For the first few weeks we were so completely absorbed in each other that we were oblivious to any reaction that our relationship had on those around us.

I was working and living on my own in the university town and it was only when I decided to take her down to Colombo to stay with my parents that it dawned on me that I was uncertain as to what sort of reception she would receive from my family.

I am the eldest of seven children and we have always found our parents glad to meet and entertain any friends we brought home. What fears I had for my girl friend were partly due to her colour and partly due to the fact that I knew my mother, like most Ceylonese women, wanted me to marry a girl of her own choice. However, I was sure I could count on my father, an avowed liberal, and very much the head of a happy family, to win round my mother.

Any fears I may have had were wholly unfounded. My parents' innate Eastern hospitality prevailed. They soon made her feel at home, my father engaging her in long conversation about England and my mother discussing new fashions in clothes with her, and stitching some lightweight dresses for her, more suitable for the hot climate. They went so far as to insist that she stayed at our home whenever she came down to Colombo. Elizabeth, a kind and naturally friendly girl, was a very difficult person to dislike. Moreover, her obvious affection for me had a strong effect on my parents.

She was completely taken in by my parents' kindness and never for a moment suspected the hidden disapproval. I could sense it only too clearly and I had to keep this to myself—the one thing that in all the time we knew each other we did not share.

What saddened me most was that, put to the test, all my father's liberal attitudes crumbled like a house of cards. The old resentment against the ruling race that had grown with him through years of colonial rule had left its indelible mark on this otherwise kind and gentle man.

Her mother fell very seriously ill and so she had to cut short her stay and hurry back home. I bought her a ring the day she left. We longed for each other as all lovers do and when her mother eventually succumbed to her illness I felt that there was now one more reason why I should be with her.

When I did come over we found that taking up from where we had left off six months before was something much sooner expressed in words than actually carried out. My first weekend at her home passed off very pleasantly. Her father and I, though at first rather shy of each other, quickly found a comforting link in his wry sense of humour, to which, I must say, I adapted myself quite easily. Her friends and relations, whom I have since come to classify as " New Statesman "-reading-Hampstead-intelligentsia, I found more difficult to take. Here were a set of people highly sophisticated and with all the right views about politics and race and religion but curiously devoid of any depth.

There was a variety of reasons that led to our final parting. She would have me join the rat-race when all I wanted was to teach classics in a secondary school in London. She would have me read the latest books and see the latest works of the in-directors and playwrights. At weekends we were to meet our friends at little parties and talk into the small hours about the latest explosion in the art world. What disillusioned her most was that, though I had the powers of vision, I was not prepared to see the light as propounded by the " New Statesman."

All this was two years ago. Today, I work as a computer programmer, live in Hampstead, and read the " Guardian."

Valentine Perera.

London SW 3.

'The Guardian'
30 May 1966

Paying Authors

Introduction

How much did authors make from books in the two-year period under survey—that is to say, volume sales plus the proceeds of subsidiary rights of the material in drama, radio, T.V., translation, serialisation, etc.? The answer is deeply disturbing—or ought to be.

Adding together both primary and secondary authors, the survey revealed that just over a sixth earned on an average more than £1,050 a year (i.e. over £20 a week), and that about one in ten earned between £550 and £1,050 a year. But the majority made much less from their books. Nearly two-thirds of them (61 per cent) averaged less than £6 a week; and as many as a third received no more than thirty shillings a week.

Recollect that most of the authors in question are not novices and hacks, but educated and experienced writers, each with a number of books to his or her credit. I hope that these figures may be assimilated by those librarians who present the author in search of a royalty on 'free' reading as a kind of pampered, ungrateful parasite. This reveals a form of gross exploitation which, in any other profession, would be recognised as a national scandal.

From 'The Book Writers', by Richard Findlater, published by The Society of Authors.

* A 'primary' author is one who puts authorship first before any other occupation, and a 'secondary' author is one who does not.

Pay Up, Gentle Reader

Ⓐ   MERVYN JONES

Two out of every three of them find that the job brings in less than a national assistance dole of £6 a week. One in three can earn only a pittance, under 30s. A few are affluent, but only one in six makes £1,000 a year. True, quite a number have other sources of income. But of those who attest that the job is their sole or chief occupation, only half can make £500 a year out of it.

Which underpaid workers are these – hospital porters, dishwashers, shoeshine men? You must have guessed; these facts relate to writers and are culled from the latest survey, *The Book Writers – Who Are They?*, cogently written by Mr Richard Findlater and published by the Society of Authors. It costs 2s. As you don't buy books, gentle reader, you probably won't buy this booklet. You have known for years that writers can't make a living, for similar reports were published by the Society and quoted in the press in 1957 and 1963, and you must also know that your refusal to buy books is the principal reason. Evidently you don't care.

Should you? Well, one doesn't expect people to care altruistically about the welfare of teachers, but one expects them to see the connection between teachers' pay and good schools. Your concern should be with the novels you get. I say novels, with due respect to other creative forms, partly because most writers and certainly most hard-up writers are novelists, but chiefly because the novel is still the mainstay of western literary culture. (Where would films and TV be without novels to cannibalise?)

It must have struck you that more good plays are written nowadays, especially by young writers, than good novels. That novel you've just finished, though clever, probably seemed shallow and trivial. The writer shied away from a deeper probing of the theme, psychological or social, which you suspect to be within his powers. Perhaps he was convincing enough if he limited himself to the doings of a few characters whose habits and background evidently reflect his own experience. But if his plot drew him to a wider environment, he appeared to lack understanding or even accurate knowledge of it. You'll have noticed that the scale of the novel is contracting, and that few modern writers tackle the task for which the form of the novel is peculiarly fitted (it's much harder to do on the stage): that is, to give a total and satisfying picture of society through many scenes and many varying characters.

You may well have noted annoying inconsistencies, both in descriptive detail and the behaviour of the characters. You may have found the style marred by clichés and by clumsy or ungrammatical sentences. To sum up, you feel that the novel is hastily written and that it might have been a work of real value if the writer had spent twice as much time on it. You are quite right. It takes a long time anyway to write a novel, and the period is doubled in length because the writer has to give half his working (I should say waking) hours to some more remunerative occupation. He isn't inclined to double the time again, for he has only one life to live. As a novelist he's working for £6 a week; the pursuit of perfection will cut his rate to £3. Research, reflection, careful writing and revision all have to be skimped. Acceptance of the second-rate is seldom conscious on the writer's part, but it is none the less real.

The novel is fast becoming a spare-time avocation, as poetry has been for decades. Poetry maintains its quality because it can be produced in fewer man-hours, and in particular because a completed work can be achieved without interruption, given a free week or even a weekend. Even so, as a total contribution to our culture it has surely suffered, both by being pushed into a mar-

ginal position, and because a poetic tradition needs its *Paradise Lost* or its *In Memoriam* as well as its lyrics. The effect of the change on the novel must be far more damaging.

One might also say that literature is becoming like local government, which depends on councillors with undemanding jobs or unearned incomes and on married (or alimony-receiving) women. Although we ought not to make the mistake of imagining that earnings are unnecessary to all women writers, or that they are more amateur in any sense than men, it remains significant that we have more women novelists than ever before. They produce a high proportion of the careful, unhurried writing that we still get – of the novels that are written, as Rosamund Lehmann has said that novels should be written, three times in longhand.

Should novelists be professionals? The cult of the amateur is cherished in England (no other country dreams of having amateur parliamentarians) and in this case is fortified by the fact that the English novel was created by part-time novelists like Defoe and Fielding. But an art form contributes most to a culture when it is broadly based, comprising many works by men of talent improved by application as well as a smaller number by men of genius. The great age of the novel in the countries where it has mattered – England, France and Russia – was an age in which both the men of talent and the men of genius, with few exceptions, were professionals.

Today the novelist cannot be a professional because he cannot earn a professional, or indeed a proletarian, income. Several adverse factors are at work, and Mr Findlater discusses them knowledgeably; but the heart of the problem is that the reading public won't buy new books. Buying paperbacks doesn't help much. Contrary to general belief, the writer's reward is slender even on a substantial sale.

Every writer is inured to being told – quite unblushingly by people with three times his income – that books are expensive. Mr Findlater has no trouble in showing that this is untrue, whether by comparison with the past or with other expenditure such as an evening at the theatre, cheerfully shouldered by the man who 'can't afford books'. Many families could buy a book a fortnight out of what they spend on newspapers and magazines.

But if British Rail were to hand out free newspapers at commuter stations to be returned at Charing Cross, who would buy a paper? I daresay people would soon convince themselves that 4d. is an exorbitant selling price. This is what has happened with books, and the public's preference for free borrowing is perfectly understandable. I will admit that when someone tells me that he's simply longing to read my new novel and has put his name down at the public library, with the manifest expectation of getting a grateful smile from me, I feel like kicking his teeth in. However, the blame does not rest on him, but on the perversion of an originally admirable institution.

Public libraries were created in the Victorian era to enable the serious-minded working man to remedy the deficiencies of his education. They contained no works of fiction; the place to borrow those was the private circulating library, which of course made a charge, and whose final demise has now brought the sales of novels to a record low. Gradually the idea took hold that literature was as valuable, and might as legitimately be studied, as biology or history, and novels were admitted to public libraries. This was clearly right; but now the thing is utterly out of hand. Novels – including quantities of crime thrillers, Westerns, sentimental romances, and what not – constitute the larger part of the stock and the issues, and are borrowed almost entirely for the sake of recreation.

I am the last person to deny that reading novels – some novels definitely, and tenably any novel – is an experience of value. But plays, films and music have a value of the same order. Very likely Mr Arnold Wesker is right in principle when he demands that all art should be free. However, it isn't. The state subsidises certain theatres, orchestras, the opera and the ballet to ensure that they should exist and that their prices should not be prohibitive. Once assured of this, the public pays and contributes to the livelihood of the artists. There is no argument for free reading which is not equally an argument for free theatres and cinemas.

Mr Findlater urges once more the scheme of charging borrowers a penny a time for the author's benefit. The justice of this proposal is obvious and the objections to it are absurd, considering that most borrowers regularly pay reservation charges and overdue fines. But the greatest benefit would go to the established author with a dozen well-known books on the shelves, not to the aspiring writer who is in real need. The question that should be asked is this: why are these new novels in the libraries instead of in the bookshops in the first place?

I suggest that they ought not to be. I further suggest (not too hopefully, but the author's penny doesn't look like winning acceptance either) a self-denying ordinance: no novel by a living author should be bought by a public library until its sale in the original edition is exhausted. This takes about a year for most novels, and the libraries would simply be doing what the paperback publishers accept as fair: giving the hardback edition a chance to sell. They

would still be free, and the principle dear to traditionalists would be preserved. People who want or need to read for nothing – whether indigent students, the old, or the stingy – would continue to do so, but they would be limited to works of information and to novels that are not new. The only difference would be for the man who's simply longing to read the latest novel. He would buy it. At least, I hope he would.

'The New Statesman'
24 July 1966

Letters to the Editor

Ⓑ Pay Up, Gentle Reader

Sir, The trouble with convincing people that novels at 21s. are cheap is that the same novels at 3s. 6d. are much cheaper. For this reason Mr Jones's analogy with theatre prices won't do. A great many people would think again about paying 30s. for a theatre ticket if they knew that in a year's time they could see the same show, with the same cast, at a sixth of the price. No argument about book buying should ignore paperbacks.

It is in connection with paperbacks that the practice of many libraries is most damaging to writers. In Mr Jones's public library (which is also mine) hundreds of paperbacks are on the shelves bound up in semi-stiff covers. From such paperbacks the author gets perhaps 3d. a copy, and for this his book goes out perhaps 30 times. Paperback publishers naturally enough disapprove of this practice, and Penguin Books actually put in a clause forbidding it, but this ban is widely ignored and apparently nobody tries to enforce it. Rebinding is so evidently and monstrously unjust to authors that no librarian tries to justify it in print.

JULIAN SYMONS

Blackheath, SE3

Ⓒ

Sir, The protests of impoverished authors should not be directed at public libraries but rather at the publishing trade. I have never bought a hard-back novel in my life; apart from the expense, they are far too bulky for convenience. Like many others I only read paperback novels. It seems to me that novelists will only get a better deal when publishers stop selling novels in bindings only suitable for libraries, and start to realise that paperbacks are what the public wants.

PETER KELSON

Middlesex

Sir, I am always amazed at the arrogance of writers such as Mervyn Jones on the subject of authors and public libraries. To suggest that the public should pay the author a hiring fee is akin to expecting us to pay a fee to the manufacturers of deck-chairs every time we hire one from Brighton Corporation to sit on the beach. The chair-maker is not concerned with what you do with the chair once you have bought it from him: why should the author claim special treatment? Most of the complaints about libraries come from authors of fiction, who claim that if the libraries didn't exist more copies of their novels would be sold. Would they? Who wants to buy a book which becomes useless after it has been read? If there were no deck-chairs for hire on Brighton beach we wouldn't buy them: we would make do with sitting on the sand.

MICHAEL SHORT
Music Librarian,
London Borough of Lambeth
London, SE24

Sir, Mr Jones says that 'the heart of the problem is that the reading public won't buy new books'. He has failed to point out that booksellers these days make it extremely difficult. A novel called *The Partnership* by Barrie Unsworth has recently been published by Hutchinson's New Authors and several extremely kind reviews induced me to go into a bookshop, have a look at his work and probably buy it. I went into at least a dozen shops over a wide area between Croydon and Eastbourne and found not one copy.

Today I decided to telephone a well-known local bookshop and order the book. I was told that to obtain books to order 'takes at least ten days'. It would have been no more trouble and may not have taken much longer for me to reserve and borrow it from my very good public library.

J. S. HAWKER

Purley, Surrey

Sir, It seems strange to chide readers for not buying an adequate number of novels while admitting that the market is glutted with the second rate, be it by necessity or want of skill. If a novelist is prepared to bestow upon the public a new piece of literature, he must accept some obligation to labour until he has created what he considers to be a reasonably finished product. The reader is weekly faced with a deluge of new novels, most of which he knows, by disheartening experience, to be second rate. To argue that if he purchased more, novelists would be able to write better books, is rather like urging people to buy rotten cabbages so that farmers would know there is a market worth improving.

MICHAEL ROBERT WELLER

Manchester

Rate for the Job

Sir, Michael Short's view that hiring out deck-chairs is in no way dissimilar from the practice of loaning books should be brought to the attention of Mr George Brown. Any librarian who is being paid more per hour than a Brighton deck-chair attendant is clearly being overpaid.

IAN RODGERS

near Aylesbury

'New Statesman'
1 July 1966

A fairer deal for authors

One of the ways in which the authors' lot could be improved would be to give him fairer tax treatment. There is a chance that at last justice may be done. Yesterday Sir Edward Boyle proposed the addition of a new clause to the Finance Bill to give limited tax relief on the sale of the copyright in an author's published works after ten years. Sir Edward later withdrew the new clause but only after the Financial Secretary to the Treasury had promised to take a closer look at the proposals put forward by the Society of Authors in terms which suggested that he might mean business. It is to be hoped that he does. The copyrights of his books are often the only assets an author has to show for a lifetime's work. It is grossly unfair that, if he tries to sell them, the proceeds are treated as current earnings.

The other suggestion by the Society of Authors, that writers should receive fees for books borrowed from a public library, needs to be considered more warily. The authors' sense of grievance is understandable. A library book may be read by dozens, even hundreds, of people, yet the author receives no more than the royalty on one copy. But free libraries have done an immense amount to spread the habit of reading and hence, too, the sales of books. In principle there may be good case for a modest charge on readers, with the benefits going in part at least to the authors of books lent. But if people were to be put off using libraries by a system of charges authors, and publishers, might finish up as losers.

'The Guardian'
13 July 1966

Authors' fees

(I) Sir,—In your leading article (July 13) on authors' fees you raise again the public lending right and conclude that this needs to be considered warily. Public libraries are not free, as anyone who has kept a book overdue knows ; nor is there any reason why they should be. A public swimming bath maintained solely from the rates charges admission fees every time one uses it. The public lending right is analogous to this. Charges for using public libraries are not a matter of principle, but of convenience.

This is where the Society of Authors has allowed itself to be outmanoeuvred. Any system of charging fees that demands that every book issued be counted and that no weight is given to who borrows the book will never work. It would cost too much to administer and it would be obviously unjust to charge such borrowers as children or pensioners.

What I would suggest is a scheme where a fee is charged at the time the borrower is registered. This would allow for these categories of borrower to be exempted. The resulting fund could then be divided among authors on a scale to be agreed between the authors and publishers. This scale could ensure that the first novel of an unknown author gets a high rate and the new novel by an established best seller a low one. If publishers supplied numbers of copies sold, this would give a rough guide to the amount of use in libraries.
—Yours sincerely,
Antony Croghan.

London, W.C.1

'*The Guardian*'
14 July 1966

Authors' fees and public lending

(J) Sir,—In reply to Mr Croghan (July 14), public lending right *is* first and foremost a matter of principle since it is an aspect of copyright which has so far been overlooked.

The Society of Authors and other organisations now represented on the working party set up by the Arts Council to study the subject, are all in agreement on this point. It is, however, true that most librarians oppose public lending right on grounds of inconvenience rather than principle ; in other words they fear the additional administrative burdens it would impose on them. To meet this difficulty a scheme whereby a fee could be charged when a borrower was registered at a public library was proposed by Sir Alan Herbert when he was conducting his campaign for public lending right. This was not acceptable to librarians.

The present proposal is to investigate the Swedish system which combines the free lending of books with the payment of royalties to the authors concerned. This seems to work well both in principle and in practice, and it is hoped to publish details of how the scheme might be adapted to British conditions in due course.—Yours truly,
M. E. Barber.
General Secretary,
The Society of Authors,
London, S.W.10

SAMPLE OF LOANS

(K) Sir,—Mr Croghan, writing on Authors' fees says : " Any system of charging fees that demands that every book issued be counted . . . will never work as it would cost too much to administer and it would be obviously unjust to charge such borrowers as children or pensioners."

Such a system is in use in one of the Scandinavian countries, and works very well. The problem of the amount to be paid to each author is solved by taking a sample of 300,000 loans, which is expressed as a fraction of the total issues of the country. The embarrassment of charging pensioners, children, and other special categories of reader (students ?) is removed by the State, which pays authors out of the Exchequer, direct.

While such a scheme has its limitations, and does not encourage new authors in the same way as the scheme advocated by Mr Croghan, it is reasonably simple and fair, being based upon the number of loans per author, which means that an author is not penalised for writing a best-seller, as he would be under Mr Croghan's scheme. Unfortunately, before such a scheme could be adopted in this country, it would need the approval of Parliament, and if present policies are maintained, this is not likely to be forthcoming.—Yours faithfully,
C. J. Eve.

Gravesend, Kent.

RETROGRADE STEP

(L) Sir,—There is every reason why public libraries should be free and it is a matter of principle.

Any introduction of charges for library use is a retrograde step. Any charge, including fines and Mr Croghan's registration fee, runs contrary to these principles and should not be considered. Joan Littlewood said recently : " Theatre shouldn't be something you pay for, it should be free like air or water or love." So should all art and so should libraries.

Nicholas C. Wilde.
London, N.W.3

'*The Guardian*'
18 July 1966

Police and Juries

Law hopelessly outdated, Lord Parker says

Ⓐ Juries discharge too many guilty men

Police and Judges alike had to act within the framework of the law, and the law was hopelessly out of date, Lord Parker of Waddington, Lord Chief Justice, said yesterday at the police college, near Basingstoke, where he inspected the officers passing out from the senior staff course.

Commenting that four out of every 10 people accused of indictable offences were acquitted in Britain, he said: " Among the four acquitted there may be an innocent man ". Under the present system, far too many guilty men were discharged, and this was due largely to the jury system.

" Many feel that the jury system has outlived its usefulness, but this country is wedded to this system and nothing will remove it.

" Just think what would happen if a Judge sitting alone acquitted a police officer. What an outcry there would be:"

Bribery attempts

In a case he took, lasting two hours, the jury was out for six and a half hours. He then discharged them. "There were 11 very angry men and one looking very complacent. I was told afterwards that the complacent man had said: ' I don't like the police and I'll never convict anyone '."

In another case attempts had been made to bribe five jurymen, "and in the sixth case I think they succeeded "

There was much to be said for giving a man's previous convictions during a case and not withholding them until or unless he was convicted. At one session 15 per cent of the jury were found to have had criminal convictions.

Greater care should be used in selecting jury members. He added: " I sometimes wonder how anyone gets convicted."

Suspended sentences

The Chief Justice of another country told him that, in his view, the only way to check the growing incidence of crime would be to give suspended sentences. " Next time ", the convicted burglar would be told, " You will lose a leg ". To the forger, for another offence: " Your right hand will come off."

Lord Parker said " we cannot do these things here ".

Among those passing out at the college were the first two women police officers ever to take the course, Woman Detective-superintendent Kathleen Skillern of Scotland Yard and Woman Superintendent Pauline Wren of Leeds, now moving to Birmingham.

'The Times'
25 June 1966

WHY THE JURY IS SLOW TO CONVICT

From Mr. Ludovic Kennedy

Sir,—In his speech to the police college (your report, June 25) Lord Parker might have added that the main reason why juries convict less than they did is because they no longer accept police evidence as readily as they did.

In recent years there has been a growing body of testimony to show that many police officers attempt to " fix " evidence, in a variety of ways, against those whom they believe to be guilty.

The 1929 Royal Commission on the Police referred to a disposition on behalf of the police " to strain the evidence against someone believed to be guilty ", and Lord Devlin, in his book, *The Criminal Prosecution in England*, says that " it is probable that responsible opinion today would reach a similar conclusion ", though he adds (in my view, wrongly) that he thinks that since then there has been a slight improvement.

Now there are two ways of dealing with this problem: Either to bury one's head in the sand, as most judges, police commissioners, &c., do, and pretend that it doesn't exist. (By the very nature of their jobs these are generally the last people to know how much it exists.) Or to admit that there is a problem, and then to ask whose fault it is, and what can be done about solving it.

If, as I think, there is much more police " fixing " of evidence than most people realize, then I submit that it is less the fault of the police than of the antiquated rules which prevent them from doing their duty. The police are hedged about with restrictions of every kind.

Why must a policeman warn a suspected man that he needn't say anything if he doesn't want to, but that, if he does, it may be taken down in writing and used in evidence ? Is not this tantamount to inviting the guilty to keep their mouths shut ? Why cannot the police have much freer powers of search ? And finally why cannot all defendants be made compellable witnesses ?

If the police knew that any man they charged would have to account for his actions in open court, they would be far less inclined than they are now to put incriminating things in his pocket or incriminating words in his mouth. I do not think that the public have any idea of the enormous psychological pressures on the police, undermanned as they are, and in the face of a soaring crime rate, to get results at almost any price. To me the wonder is not that so many policemen succumb, but that so many more do not.

If, as we say, we want the police to get a real grip on crime, then it is our duty to give them greater powers to enable them to do so. They are dealing for the most part with wicked and ruthless men. If we do not do this, they will continue to be tempted to take the law into their own hands; and we must not be surprised if at times innocent men are convicted and, too often, as Lord Parker says, guilty ones get off.

Yours, &c.,
LUDOVIC KENNEDY.

Roxburghshire.

'The Times'
29 June 1966

From Major Sir John Ferguson

Sir,—The Lord Chief Justice has emphasized the fact that four out of every 10 people accused of indictable offences are acquitted in Britain after trial by jury and has commented that " Among the four acquitted there may be an innocent man " (*The Times*, June 25).

May a retired police officer offer two practical suggestions which may reduce the risk of improper acquittal while preserving the principle that a jury must be " sure " of guilt before they convict ?

Experience of criminal trials prompts the reflection that the cherished " privilege of silence "—the rule that no man is bound to incriminate himself—is a fertile source of improper acquittals.

The " Judges' Rules " which are designed to give detailed guidance to police officers in taking statements from suspected persons are founded upon this privilege and require a police officer to administer a " caution " as soon as he has evidence which would afford reasonable grounds for suspecting that a person has committed an offence.

It is not possible, within the scope of a letter to you, to describe the formidable and treacherous obstacle which these rules can place in the path of a police officer seeking to carry out his duty in investigating a crime. The interests of the accused could be—and are—adequately safeguarded by excluding from the evidence against him any statement which is induced by threats or duress. If the " Judges' Rules " were revoked the police would be relieved of an impractical fetter on their work and of a temptation to impropriety.

Another occasional but significant cause of improper acquittals also stems from the " privilege of silence "; the right of an accused person against whom a judge has ruled there is " a case to answer " to abstain from giving evidence instead of answering it in the witness box.

If such persons were required to submit to cross-examination criminal trials before a jury would be less liable to error.

As Jeremy Bentham wrote of the privilege of silence in 1825:—" If all criminals of every class had assembled, and framed a system after their own wishes, is not this rule the very first which they would have established for their security ? Innocence never takes advantage of it; innocence claims the right of speaking, as guilt invokes the privilege of silence."

Can we in 1966 afford to ignore these words in the circumstances to which the Lord Chief Justice has drawn attention ? Is not the answer that the " privilege of silence " must go ?

I am, Sir, yours faithfully,
J. F. FERGUSON.

Rye, Sussex.

'The Times'
30 June 1966

INTEGRITY OF THE POLICE

From the Chief Constable of Hertfordshire

Sir,—In his letter today Mr. Ludovic Kennedy expresses his concern that the existing rules of evidence allow too many guilty criminals to escape conviction. It is regrettable that in putting forward helpful suggestions by way of remedy Mr. Kennedy should make an unwarranted attack on the integrity of the police.

What support can he find for his assertion that in recent years there has been a growing body of testimony to show that many police officers attempt to " fix " evidence ? By training and tradition the police in this country accept it as their duty to protect the rights of the individual and unfair treatment of an accused person is condemned by all ranks.

Mr. Kennedy's opinion that " police commissioners, &c.", by the very nature of their jobs are the last persons to know how much malpractice exists shows a lack of appreciation of the real responsibilities of senior police officers. His view is not shared by those who have troubled to inform themselves of the facts.

In 1962 the Royal Commission on the Police, after hearing a large number of witnesses from all sections of the community, reported : " The foregoing evidence gives us no reason to doubt that chief constables and senior officers are, in general, scrupulously fair and thorough in investigating complaints against their members." It is safe to say that no professional body in this country is more painstaking than the police in investigating complaints against their members.

The police are rightly jealous of their reputation and of the high standard of conduct they maintain. The constant repetition of irresponsible allegations and insinuations does a grave disservice to the police and is bitterly resented by a body of men who deserve the confidence and the support of the public.

I am, Sir, your obedient servant,
A. F. WILCOX, President of the Association of Chief Police Officers.
Chief Constable's Office, Hatfield, Hertfordshire, June 29.

'The Times'
1 July 1966

WHY THE JURY IS SLOW TO CONVICT

From Mr. J. P. Eddy, Q.C.

Sir,—As one who has followed the administration of justice in this country for more than half a century I find myself unable to accept the proposition put forward by Mr. Ludovic Kennedy (June 29) that juries no longer accept police evidence as readily as they did.

The suggestion that many police officers attempt to " fix " evidence is, I believe, an exaggeration. That an officer occasionally presses a case unduly against a defendant whom he believes to be guilty, and indeed may even go further, may well be true. I can only say that I have no personal knowledge of any such cases. But my own impression is that out of the thousands of officers who compose our police there are surprisingly few who let down their highly responsible calling.

People who condemn our juries for acquitting so-called guilty men overlook the inevitable disadvantage under which they discharge their duties. Unlike our judges and the police, they usually know nothing of the record of the person whom they may be trying. Unless the accused puts his character in issue they are restricted and, I think, rightly restricted, to the evidence relevant to the charge before them, and as a rule they do not know whether he has been in trouble previously or not.

This may well explain why so-called guilty men are occasionally let off. But I cannot believe it would be a good thing to make a prisoner's record available to the jury. Too often he would be tried on that rather than on the evidence concerning the charge against him.

I agree that the Judges' Rules, which were revised two years ago, need further revision. By the law of the land, no confession is admissible unless it is " free and voluntary ", and I believe that the rules are largely superfluous. Certainly I think that in some cases they hamper the police unduly.

Mr. Ludovic Kennedy's proposal that all defendants should be made compellable witnesses is quite impracticable. Supposing the defendant refuses to give evidence —what do we do with him? Do we subject him to torture as in olden days?

We should be slow to tamper with our system of justice, which I believe enjoys the admiration of the world, even if occasionally " guilty " men get off. At present, jurors are told that before they can convict they must be satisfied of the guilt of the accused " beyond reasonable doubt ", and it will be a poor day for English justice when the law permits a lower standard of proof.

Yours faithfully,
J. P. EDDY.

Temple, London, E.C.4

'The Times'
2 July 1966

TRIAL BY JURY

From Mr. R. T. Oerton

Sir,—Mr. Ludovic Kennedy (June 29) adds his voice to the growing chorus of those concerned at the number of accused men acquitted by the courts. He attributes this state of affairs to juries' doubts about police evidence, these doubts to the frequency of police " fixing " and this " fixing " in turn to the technical rules by which the police are hamstrung.

Some of these technicalities are certainly designed not so much to protect the innocent as to give the guilty a sporting chance of escape, and they are more appropriate to the grouse moors than to the criminal courts. But they should be viewed within the context of the penal system as a whole.

This still remains primarily punitive rather than preventive, geared to punish wickedness rather than to the prevention of crime. Far too many criminals are subjected to an unimaginative and unconstructive punitive regime with no reformative and little deterrent value. In fact they act as scapegoats for the repudiated feelings and failings of society as a whole, and so long as we continue to treat them as scapegoats it is natural for us to give a sporting chance of escape to those in danger of having to play the role.

Sitting birds should not be shot; but a sitting bird which has been causing damage may reasonably be apprehended in an attempt to cure it, as humanely as possible, of its harmful propensities. If technicalities are to be abolished, a rational humanity should replace them.

Yours faithfully,
R. T. OERTON.

Poole, Dorset.

'The Times'
3 July 1966

' NEW ATTITUDE TO CRIME '

From Mr. L. P. Hartley

Sir,—The unwillingness of juries to convict is, of course, one cause of the increase in crime. Many others have been suggested, e.g., the various forms of public entertainment which invest crime with glamour.

But there are two, seldom mentioned, which seem to me no less important. One is the training of Commando troops which, during the war and since, has acted as an incitement to violence; and the other, more subtle and pervasive, is what has been called the " new attitude to crime ".

The new attitude to crime amounts to an excuse for crime as being something outside the individual's control. In some quarters it is accepted that crime is a mental illness. The theories of Freud have helped to undermine the idea of Free Will, and the plea of " diminished responsibility ", which has found its way into the Statute Book, has also helped. In the domain of morals no saying is more popular than " There but for the Grace of God go I ", with its implication that we must not sit in judgment.

The Home Secretary has said that he wishes for " a tolerant society ". But tolerant of what? Surely not of murder and crimes of violence? If a policeman slips up he gets called over the coals; yet no one has a better right to plead " diminished responsibility " than the policeman, whose nerves are always on the stretch and whose self-control is continually threatened by the kind of people, and acts, he has to deal with.

Yours faithfully,
L. P. HARTLEY.

Assissi, Italy, July 4

'The Times'
11 July 1966

From Mr. Christopher Besley

Sir,—Your correspondent Mr. L. P. Hartley (July 11) is no doubt correct in blaming the training of troops in wartime for part of the increase in crimes of violence, and the " new attitude to crime " for another part of that increase.

A new attitude to crime against property also arose during wartime as a result of certain items of Service equipment being classified as " expendable ", a word which became synonymous with " belonging to anyone who wanted it ".

Since in one sense all Service equipment is public property the attitude was extended to many items which were useful to the individual and which were acquired by a process described as " winning ", which was widely regarded as not being criminal and was not adequately discouraged as such.

This attitude persisted into the peace and attached not only to nationalized and governmental bodies but also to the many giant corporations, many of whose employees regarded themselves as entitled as of right to " perks ". These same employees who would not steal from " Mr. Jones, the butcher " would regard shoplifting from a supermarket or defrauding the railway or some other faceless corporation as being nearer to a win on the pools than to the crime of larceny.

The conclusion would appear to be that the increase in public ownership and the trend towards larger and larger corporations diminishes the public consciousness of the meaning of private property and the laws relating to its protection.

I am, Sir, your obedient servant,
CHRISTOPHER BESLEY.

London, S.W.19

'The Times'
13 July 1966

From Mr. Evan Davies

Sir,—Mr. L. P. Hartley may have made some valid points in his letter today but his suggestion that one of the more important factors in the increase of crime is " the training of Commando troops during the war and since ", implies that the ranks of criminals have been filled by ex-Commandos. This must be refuted at once.

Commando training is an extension of basic army training and those who receive it generally possess the very qualities a criminal lacks, i.e., sense of responsibility, self-discipline and intelligence.

Mr. Hartley may not know that some 500 police officers volunteered for Commando service during the war and, as one of them who has since been engaged in suppressing crime, I can assure him that the ex-Commando in the dock is a rarity.

Yours faithfully,
EVAN M. DAVIES.

London, W.2, July 11

Problems of the Aged

PROBLEM OF THE AGED WHO
Ⓐ   LIVE AND DIE ALONE

A few mornings ago Mrs. B, who is crippled by arthritis, slipped and fell as she got out of bed. She recalls that as she lay helpless for nearly five hours, she kept repeating " Please God, help me to get up."

Mrs. B lives alone in a first-floor room cluttered with her possessions. Because she cannot manage the stairs she has not left the house for seven years, and she never sees the other people living there. Luckily she was found by a council worker who comes in daily to do her shopping and help with the chores.

Luckily, because she might have been one of the many thousands of old people who are never visited, who live in squalor, and who may die without anyone knowing for days afterwards. Eventually someone's suspicions are aroused by drawn curtains or uncollected milk bottles and the police are called.

In Leeds last year, according to the Chief Constable's annual report, 101 people were found dead and 48 ill or injured. This in a city with a population of just over 500,000 and in the north where neighbourly ties are said to be stronger than elsewhere.

Taken by itself, the Leeds figure implies that at least 5,000 people in Britain may die alone and neglected every year; that perhaps 20 times as many are living in circumstances where such a thing could easily happen. Nobody knows the real figure for the whole country.

Every week

In Birmingham the coroner's office have dealt with a number of such cases over the past few years. No exact figures are available. Nor are there in Liverpool, a city of close and friendly communities, where the coroner's office get " quite a fair number " in a year.

In neither city would the numbers come near those given by a coroner's officer in one part of London. He told *The Times* that every week he deals with the cases of at least two or three old people who are found dead, without neighbours having any idea that anything was wrong. His district has a population of 130,000, including a fairly high percentage of elderly people living alone.

" In the many cases I come across ", he said, " the time lapse between death and someone discovering it may be anything from a couple of days to a month or even more."

Often a post mortem shows that the person may have been in considerable pain during the last days, and incapable of calling for help.

The same coroner's officer said that many of the lonely people found dead had children or grandchildren living. " When we trace them and break the news ", he added, " they often show no particular concern."

Could he suggest a solution ? He said: " It is a difficult problem. There is no shortage of volunteers for the more interesting kinds of welfare work, but looking after old people is not particularly pleasant."

Local councils and the various voluntary organizations cannot cope with this problem of people dying alone and unheeded. Relations between council welfare departments and other bodies are generally fairly good, and they refer some cases to each other. Leaflets printed by the Westminster City Council, for instance, mention services provided by the Red Cross and W.V.S., but only a fraction of the old people in any district can be visited regularly.

Help refused

Even if enough social workers were available, there would still be a big problem in finding those in need of help. Many impoverished old people live in single rooms on upper floors or in basements, and some, ill or crippled, cannot answer the door.

Many are fiercely independent and resent anything that sounds like charity. They refuse offers of a home-help, decline to draw national assistance. They have a horror of being sent to a home.

Since only the police have powers of forcible entry, such people often cannot be reached until it is too late.

The idea that young people had a duty to care for their aged relatives has largely disappeared. Slum clearance and rehousing have broken up old communities and there have been many complaints of the impersonal loneliness of tall blocks of flats. Old people's housing projects, with rows of self contained bungalows, are still a comparative rarity.

Perhaps the most imaginative project to overcome public indifference is Task Force, conceived by a young barrister, Mr. Anthony Steen. He has organized hundreds of young volunteers in London, many still at school, to visit the old and the lonely, and has raised several thousand pounds from various sources, including the Government.

Ironically, the Government contribution is a development grant for young people from the Department of Education and Science. None of the Ministries directly concerned with the elderly and the ill was able to provide any money.

The youngsters have concentrated on befriending old people—talking to them, running errands, playing games, doing domestic chores and repairs and arranging outings for instance—and often have succeeded where professional social workers might be resented.

Some local authorities have been cooperative and encouraging. Others have wanted nothing to do with the scheme. Even some of the voluntary organizations have received it coldly.

'The Times'
6 June 1966

(B)

From Mrs. Sheila Bull.

Sir,—Your article " Problems of the aged who live and die alone " (June 6) states ' . . . Old people's housing projects, with rows of self-contained bungalows, are still a comparative rarity." What a very good thing that they *are* so rare !

There is nothing quite so depressing as an outwardly sparkling looking little estate of " purpose-built bungalows for old people ". The very infirm cannot get help from their elderly neighbours : the more active but none the less aged members loathe the quiet, absence of children, and aura of death.

Most elderly people are not afraid of death, but they do not want to be reminded of it constantly, without the leavening influence of new babies coming into the community.

I do not believe that segregation of the elderly is a good thing : as your article indicates, the greatest help for them comes from youngsters.

Integration should be the aim, not segregation. The latter is a retrograde step, too reminiscent of the days when the mentally sick, lepers, and other embarrassments were banished from the general community.

Yours faithfully,
SHEILA BULL.

London, N.10

'The Times'
13 June 1966

(C)

From Lord Gage

Sir,—I do not know from what experience or authority Mrs. Sheila Bull seeks to denigrate purpose-built bungalows for the elderly (June 13).

It falls to my lot to visit a number of such homes erected and managed by voluntary housing associations, and I have never yet failed to find the greatest gratitude among the tenants for the accommodation and services provided.

This is not entirely surprising seeing that the giving of satisfaction to these elderly tenants is the sole motive and incidentally reward of those who devote so much time and effort to establishing these homes.

Indeed, if anyone were to accompany me on these visits, I think they would go away with only one criticism, and that is there ought to be many many more of these homes.

I am, Sir, your obedient servant,

GAGE, President, National Federation of Housing Societies.
Lewes, Sussex.

(D)   ### Integration

From Mr. Daniel Schonfield

Sir,—How right Mrs. Sheila Bull is when she says (June 13) in relation to the housing of elderly people that integration should be the aim, not segregation.

We, of the Samaritan Housing Association, formed to provide just this type of accommodation, have had the truth of her statement amply demonstrated in our pilot scheme at Arthur Bliss House, Lindfield.

There we have four married couples and 16 widows and widowers. All of them have their own self-contained flats where they can live their own lives in their own way, and all of them can meet together in a large well-furnished lounge to watch television, play cards, or just talk.

But what is of particular interest is that Arthur Bliss House is part of a private enterprise housing estate. In several cases the residents are the parents of the young couples who have bought a house on the estate, thus enabling the aging parents to retain independence but, at the same time, keeping the family close together.

We have found that our elderly residents enjoy acting as baby-sitters for the young couples and, on the other hand, the couples enjoy dropping in to Arthur Bliss House for a cup of coffee and a chat. This life for the elderly is as it should be, and it is a pity that there is not more of it.

Yours faithfully,
DANIEL SCHONFIELD, Chairman,
Samaritan Housing Association Limited.

Twickenham, Middlesex.

'The Times'
16 June 1966

Mental ward rescue plan

 (E)   **by a Staff Reporter**

PROJECT 70—a plan to rescue mentally normal old people from the wards of mental hospitals—has been launched by a new London society, Aid for the Elderly in Government Institutions (AEGIS), whose chairman is Lord Strabolgi.

The plight of the old people, who have been placed in mental institutions because there was no room for them elsewhere, has been described by the Minister of Health, Mr Kenneth Robinson, as " undesirable," and plans for more geriatric wards have been drawn up by the Ministry.

Doors locked

AEGIS has distressing evidence of the plight of old people inside mental hospitals. The presence of one or two violent patients in a ward may mean that doors are kept locked and teeth and spectacles taken away. In rare cases the lack of staff means that a physical disability is ignored, or worse. Some drugs produce extreme thirst, but old people may be incontinent; if drink is refused them because of this, the only available water has to be scooped from the lavatory pan.

As a first step the society wants hospitals to sort out the normal from the insane ; a difficult and lengthy process, since it would mean a complete rediagnosis (and would call in question the diagnosis which led to certification in the first place).

Houses and flats

Then it would like to see existing buildings razed and their grounds used to build special accommodation for the elderly, side by side with houses and flats for ordinary people. The society has calculated that the average density of the 30 London mental hospitals surveyed so far stands at 10 beds per acre.

Mr Peter Thomson, AEGIS planning consultant, thinks that building the new communities on hospital sites in London would provide accommodation for at least 200,000 people. The scale and continuity of such a plan would also provide an unrivalled opportunity for the development of industrialised building techniques.

'The Observer'
4 September 1966

QUESTIONS

Note to Teachers

The following questions are not intended to be comprehensive; they merely represent the sort of investigation that we personally think is most profitable.

More important, they are worded as briefly as possible. In this form they are perhaps more useful to the teacher than to the pupil, since only the most able pupils would be able to cope with them directly. We envisage that teachers will wish to rephrase the questions to suit the occasion, or perhaps to draw attention to some points in a more direct and simple way.

School till 16

A. It is possibly true that Sir Edward Boyle would not like to teach a class of unwilling 15-year-olds. If so, is this fact in any way relevant to the argument?

B. Is it a *fact* or a *reasonable guess* or a *wild speculation* that larger classes mean less individual progress?
Who said the present system works efficiently?

C. Is it fair to compare hospitals and schools in this way?

D. Why do you think C. N. Wright sent this letter?

E. & F. To what extent do the writers of these two letters agree?

G. On what grounds does R. Torbett condemn the views of V. L. Coombes? How does he make a personal issue of the argument?
Why does he think a school in Bovey Tracey is sure to be 'comfortable'?

H. & I. How would G. A. Muirhead prove the 'undisputable fact' that some children cannot benefit from further formal education? Does K. W. Ruddiman successfully overcome the argument in letter H.?

J. How would you describe Peter Simple's attitude to this problem? Imagine that a person in favour of raising the school leaving age was annoyed by the article. What sort of criticism could he *fairly* make?

Drinking Laws

A. Why do you think the editor published this letter?

B. The writer says that there is no doubt that our drinking laws increase drunkenness instead of restricting it. How could you find out if this is the case? If it *is* the case, what explanation might exist?
Why does he talk about a whole family taking refreshments together? Is this in connexion with laws to do with licencing hours, or has he a different law (to do with age) in mind?
Do many people really think it is *sinful* to drink between 3 p.m. and 6 p.m. in this country? Why does he use that word? How is it different in meaning from *illegal*?

What kind of laws, apart from drinking laws, might the writer suspect of being based on the 'intolerance of a minority'? What minority might he suspect has the power to keep the present drinking laws? If the majority of people in this country wanted to change the drinking laws, could they do so?
Does the fact (?) that it is harder to find drunkenness in Belgium *prove* that there is *actually* less drunkenness? How could the absence in Belgium of a fixed 'closing-time' make it harder to find drunkenness?

C. Do you think that the writer would expect *all* types of shops to stay open at all hours to suit his convenience?
With whom is the writer arguing when he says: 'It would be nonsense to say that we could not alter our drinking laws'?
Is a system which works perfectly well on the Continent bound to work here? What exactly does the writer mean by 'works perfectly well'?

E. What does the writer think has caused road accidents to increase since the lengthening of licencing hours? How could one *prove* whether this connection existed or not?
Is there any real conflict between the views expressed in letters B. and E.?
Does one *only* have to read of the increased road accidents to realise . . . ?

Minority Language

A. Why does Mrs. Cardy use the word 'smattering'?
Would she object less if the children learned to speak Welsh *fluently*? Would she think it a waste of time to acquire a 'smattering' of Russian or French?

B. Is the teaching of English to immigrant Pakistanis strictly comparable with the case in question?
Does Alan Howard have any grounds for supposing that Mrs. Herbert holds the views expressed in the last sentence?

C. Why is Welsh taught in Welsh schools, according to Mrs. MacBean?
Discuss what is meant by a parent's right 'to choose within reason how his child is educated'.

General

Supposing that your family moved to Wales, what arguments could your parents give for/against your learning Welsh?

Dressing Up for the Wedding

A.   Why does Mary Stott use the word 'mob' rather than 'lots' in the first paragraph? What does she mean by 'pretentious public charade'?

What does she mean by 'us' and 'our' in paragraph 6?

Do you think she would herself be in favour of brides sending a note as described in the last paragraph? Why does she mention Oxfam?

Discuss any words which express prejudice, like '*ludicrously inappropriate*'). What positive case does she make against expensive weddings?

B.   How good a case for wearing a white gown is made in paragraph 2?

Discuss the use of the words 'decent' and 'clinical'.

Why does the writer really favour church weddings? Does religion come into it?

C. What is an 'agnostic *conviction*'?

D. Explain why Derek Smith would not be in favour of sending money to Oxfam instead of spending it on elaborate weddings.

E. How strong a case in favour of church weddings is given here? If it turned out that there was a higher divorce rate among people married in register offices than among those married in churches, would this *in fact* support the writer's argument? Or would there be a more obvious explanation?

F   Does it seem likely to you that elaborate weddings encourage many early marriages? Is there any way of testing this theory?

G. Is it unreasonable for a girl to say: 'Even though I am an agnostic, I'll marry in church to please my mother, who has done so much to help me. But I draw the line at having my children baptised, even to please her'?

General

Probably the editor of *The Guardian* received many more letters on this subject, though these are all that were printed. What factors probably influenced his selection of letters?

Factory Farming

A.   What points made by Ruth Harrison specifically criticise factory farming and *not* situations which could occur in connection with *any* kind of farming?

The writer of F. says Ruth Harrison's article is full of 'emotive words'. Give some examples, and discuss to what extent the force of her argument depends on them.

B.   What parts of this letter seem to you to fairly answer points made by Ruth Harrison? If possible, read her book, *Animal Machines*, so that you can appreciate the full extent of this controversy.

Does anything seem strange about D. Sainsbury's use of the word 'imposed' in the last paragraph but one?

C.   Is it true that the two attitudes mentioned by the writer are 'completely opposed'?

Discuss the full meaning of the last sentence. Is it supported by any facts in Ruth Harrison's article?

F.   How effective a reply is this to points made in A.? How might Ruth Harrison reply?

G.   Comment on the use of the word 'natural' in paragraph 2.

Would it have been sensible for the first settled agriculturalists to be criticised by hunting nomads for domesticating animals and thereby robbing them of their 'natural freedom'? Try to defend such a point of view. What is the difference between this and the attitude of the writer of this letter?

Discuss the full implications of the last sentence.

H.   Are these the only two answers?

I.   Is this analogy a fair one?

School Meals

A. What is the writer's case for saying that children should not have a school dinner if it could be provided at home? What is her case for saying that if they do stay, they should pay the full cost of the meal? Would she agree that prosperous mothers whose children *have* to stay to school dinners should also pay the full cost?

B. & D. What is probably the main reason for Mr. Taylor's dislike of the school meal service? Why does he think that schools should not cater for 'the convenience of mothers'?

Does Mrs. Schofield make a better case against providing meals at school?

C. & E. Do these letters succeed in making a good case for continuing the school meals service?

F. Would the fact that the school meal service was *overstrained* justify introducing the scheme suggested here? What other facts could be used to justify the scheme?

G. Is this an effective criticism of the last paragraph of letter A.?

General

How have the opinions of the various writers been influenced by their position as teacher or parent? Which of the other letters directly answer points made in Letter A.?

Issues discussed in these letters are:
  a) should children be allowed to stay if they could be fed at home?

b) should an economic price (2s. 6d.) be paid by all parents who can afford it?

c) should teachers have to supervise school meals when this could be done by unskilled staff?

d) is there any variation of methods of dispensing school meals which would improve matters?

How clearly does each letter stick to one or more of these distinct issues?

The Great Train Robbery

A. Could one logically admire the 'skill and courage' behind the great train robbery, and yet still believe the robbers should be severely punished?

Could one logically say: 'I deplore the 30-year sentence, but I still think it would be bad if the prisoners escaped during the term of imprisonment?

What 'jump' is made between the question in paragraph 4 and the statement in paragraph 5?

B. Is it true that Mr. Greene condemns the severity of the sentences because it was *bank* money that was stolen?

Would it be silly to say: 'I heartily sympathise with the victims of robberies, but still think 30 years is too severe a punishment?

Discuss the meaning and force of the word 'salutary' as used here.

What is taken for granted in the expression 'Thugs they are, and as thugs they should be treated'?

C. & F. Discuss the conflict of opinion in these two letters. What different ideas do they imply about the purpose of punishment?

Which makes the better contribution to thought on this important subject?

D. & E. Is it worse to assault law-abiding citizens than others?

Major Howard uses 'cowardly' to describe the assault. Why?

He accuses Mr. Greene of vindictiveness. Against whom?

How does he try to show that Greene cannot think logically?

Why does Major Howard suppose that Mr. Greene's 'hero-worship' of criminals is a major cause of delinquency? Is that what he really meant to say?

Which letter is the more useful contribution to the argument, D. or E.?

General

Which letters most reflect the writer's

a) job

b) political views

c) emotions

d) constructive thought?

Maria Marten

D. Should it be possible for one to be completely in sympathy with Marian Stringer's sentiments, and yet still find this production 'hilariously funny'?

E. Is it true, do you think, that Miss Stringer's *moral or religious* susceptibilities were outraged? Or do you think she may have been offended in some quite different sort of way?

Is it fair of Mr. Forder to imply that Miss Stringer is not entitled to protest because she made no effort to prevent the production?

How good a case does Mr. Forder make in dismissing the three charges? Do you agree that these are, in fact, the main charges made or implied by Miss Stringer?

Can one fully agree with Mr. Forder, yet still sympathise with Miss Stringer's views?

Boarding and Day Schools

A. How good a case does the writer make against sending children to boarding schools? Apart from her 'central point' (see last paragraph) which other of her objections would apply to an up-to-date boarding school?

The writer anticipates some of the pro-boarding-school arguments that her article might provoke. Which ones?

B. Why do you think the editor printed this letter on the same page as A.?

What assumptions does the writer make about a) grammar school buildings as opposed to secondary modern buildings; b) grammar school girls' general behaviour; c) grammar school teachers; d) the type of school attended by children of readers of *The Guardian*; e) the diet of middle-class (as opposed to working-class) children; f) the effect of comprehensive education on ex-grammar school pupils?

Are these assumptions justified? How could they be tested?

D. Does the fact that many children enjoy boarding school life conflict with anything said by Gillian Tindall? (See also F.)

Is to send one's child to a boarding school 'gradually to renounce one's authority over one's children and *allow them to create a life of their own*'?

Can paragraph 5 be checked in practice?

Find out who Joy Baker is. What is the point of the reference?

E. What does the writer think the Government could do to 'improve' this situation?

G. Precisely what harm does the writer think might come to the secondary modern school she describes if it became part of a comprehensive school?

Agricultural Sprays

B. What 'official quarters' does he mean?

In what sense is the word 'crimes' being used in the last paragraph?

C. & D. How far does the evidence quoted justify the grim predictions made by these writers?

E. How fair is the writer's comparison of this case with those who have 'received injuries assisting the police'?

Is the case for 3rd Party Insurance a good one?

How could the writer support his statement that legislation is delayed by Parliament's 'obsession with sex and trivialities'? Some people will drag 'sex' into *any* discussion to draw attention to themselves. Is this what Mr. Hills is doing in this unlikely context? Does he *really* mean to imply that 'sex' is trivial?

G. Why does the writer refer to 'the C.N.D. people'?

H. Did the Ministry have reason on its side?

K. Is Peter Simple directly attacking any particular products?

Is this article meant only to amuse those who in any case agree with him or is it aimed also at changing the views of those who *disagree* with him?

General
Which letters are the most helpful and constructive?

Reporting Violence

A. Why is Dr. Fox convinced that there should be much less reporting of violence, when he admits that 'no one can yet prove this thing for certain'?

Discuss the two analogies in the last paragraph.

What would be the practical effect of a decision by newspapers to include no reports of violence until it had been proved that such reports were harmless?

B. In what way does the article *factually* misrepresent Dr. Fox?

How would Dr. Fox reply to the criticisms implied in paragraphs 3, 4 and 5?

C. Does this letter successfully answer paragraphs 2 and 3 in B?

D. In what respects does Harry Whewell agree with Dr. Fox?

How good a case does he make for newspapers devoting some space to the *straight* reporting of trials? How important to his argument is the distinction between 'straight' and 'coloured' reporting?

E. Discuss the significance of the information given about space devoted to the Moors trial in various newspapers.

Discuss the implications of the last sentence. Would it follow that no act of violence should *ever* be shown on T.V. if *one* child might imitate it?

F. Dr. Fox points out elsewhere that the kind of person most likely to be affected by reported violence is *not* likely to be known to a mental hospital, and that patients in such hospitals are a comparatively small danger in this respect. Does this point answer that made in paragraph 2 of this letter?

How good a point is the writer making in his last paragraph?

G. Do *newspapers* always give prominence to events of national importance or could Mr. Davies be equally critical of them?

General
In which cases may the writer's views be affected by his profession?

Remembrance Days.

A. Could it be argued that, even if one favoured the use of A-bombs in the war, uprooting the cherry trees was an objectionable act? How good a case does the Canon make for the use of the A-bomb?

B. Why does the writer think our educational system is totally futile?

How would the writer justify his statement: 'For many hundreds of years philosophers and historians have not said one word worth saying'?

C. Why does the writer say that she 'thanked God for the lives of those who have in the past won freedom for us'? Is she saying
   a) that it is good to have remembrance days but silly to have two minutes silence, or
   b) the whole idea of remembrance days is futile, if people are too young to remember?

General
What questions would you put to the Canon, and to the other writers, if you wanted to explore their attitudes further?

Gas, Electricity and Landscape

C. *Is* it reasonable to expect these sub-stations to be individually designed?

If it is true that only a few people condemn the pylons, etc., has this minority any right to object?

Could the number of abandoned cars in the countryside be taken as a measure of the country's rising living standards? Comment on the third paragraph of this letter.

D. It is not possible in this book to state fairly the case made by the Electricity Board. You could obtain several leaflets from the Board which would help you to see the problems involved, and to appreciate the amount of thought that is given to protecting the landscape.

What part of D answers points made in letter B ?

Is the comparison in the last paragraph a fair one ?

E., F. & G.   Some factors mentioned are:
    a) the number of people who visit a particular area
    b) literary associations
    c) scenic beauty
    d) cost and convenience of carrying electricity.

How is it possible to decide which are the most important ? Discuss the claims made in these three reports. Compare the two claims made in G.

Warnings to Children

Both A. and B. are aimed at discouraging children from placing themselves in danger. To gain their effect they have to risk the possibility of making children *unreasonably* afraid of strangers. Is this risk justifiable ? Is there any way in which it could be discovered whether the warnings do more good than harm ?

Do you agree with Margaret Rickards about the motive of the writer of *The Death of a Father* ? Could a *good* poem on the same subject have the effect of making children more appreciative of their parents ? What is there about this particular poem which is likely to make children feel 'got at' ?

Marrying Young

A.   If John Grigg's views are correct, what practical measures do you think he would suggest as a means of discouraging early marriage ?

B.   Is it true that John Grigg overlooked 'the tendency to start courtship early' as a factor encouraging early marriages ?

Comment on the writer's use of the word 'leap' in the second paragraph.

What practical measures would the writer suggest to 'reverse the fashion' ?

C. Discuss the full meaning of the sentence: 'Divorce does not result from young marriages, but from the defects in our social system, of which the tendency to marry younger is but a symptom'.

What defects may he be referring to ?

D.   What steps of reasoning have led from the quotation in paragraph 3 to the statement in paragraph 5 ?

Would it be unreasonable to say: 'Most people under the age of 21 are too immature emotionally to be sure of starting a successful marriage ? Nevertheless, many factors make it desirable to lower the age at which one can marry without parental consent' .

What would be the significant factors ?

General

Why does the *Sunday Mirror* present this material in very short paragraphs ?

Genesis

A. The article expresses (among other things) the idea that whereas mankind can destroy itself, only God can bring the dead to life.

Is the article aimed at
    a) proving there is a God
    b) proving that God would not forgive the person responsible for destroying Mankind
    c) illustrating the dangers of excessive pride on the part of scientists
    d) proving that atheism is dangerous
or e) making any other point ?
What do you think *is* the main point ?

B, Was it, in fact, suggested that the Prime Minister was an atheist ?

C. What is blasphemy ? Why does the writer think that Brian Morris was being blasphemous ? What 'dearly held convictions' of Alan Gamble may have been affronted ? (The writer of B. is also a Roman Catholic.)

Could it be argued that Brian Morris was *attacking* blasphemy ?

D. What 'tone of reality' does the writer refer to ?

Would any of the virtues described in paragraph 2 *necessarily* conflict with the verdict of blasphemy ?

General

Does Brian Morris intend to influence the reader's *political* views in any way ?

The New Morality

A.   Does Sir Cyril Black believe that the BBC is responsible for all the views expressed in its programmes ?

Does he think that the 'two new commandments' are bad ones ? Why does he quote them ?

Whom does he mean by 'the nation' in the last paragraph ?

By what means does he show his disapproval of all the medical biologist's views ?

B.   What does the writer mean by 'intellectuals' ?

What sort of evidence could be given to defend his last sentence ?

D.   In what sense does the writer use the word 'Christian' ? Does this differ from what M. O. Goodman would mean by this word ?

Discuss his use of the word 'commonsense'.

E. Does it appear that the writer is for, or against, the 'new morality' ?

F. Mr. Loxton gives the 'real' meaning of the 'new commandments'. Do you think that Dr. Comfort would at all object to the new phrasing?

What evidence would the writer give to show that Christian love and self-discipline are 'the only secure basis for society'? Does he mean *any* society, or just *our* society?

General

Which of these writers makes the most *constructive* comments on the subject?

Two Sorts of Colour Problem

As far as you can tell, what were the main reasons for these two friendships breaking up?

Consider the following *possible* factors in relation to each writer:

    a) difference of education
    b) difference of parents' social status
    c) difference of personal habits
    d) difference of taste and interests

By reading between the lines, is it possible to guess any other factors that might have been important?

Paying Authors

A. Why does Mervyn Jones think libraries should not stock new novels? Why does he think that this would be a better idea than charging borrowers a penny for each book?

Is there any evidence available to support the idea that novelists would write better books if they had more money?

Is Mervyn Jones mainly concerned that authors should be paid a *living* wage or a *fair* wage?

B. According to Julian Symons, why is it more damaging to a writer for the library to stock paper-back editions than to stock hard-backed editions?

Does it affect the argument how many times the book is borrowed?

C. Why does Peter Kelson think novelists would get a better deal if only paper-backs were sold?

D. Can the chair-maker fairly be compared with the writer? Would nobody buy books if there were no libraries? Do books become useless after they are read?

E. How might Mervyn Jones reply to this letter?

H. How could writers and publishers suffer as a result of a charge to borrowers from libraries?

I., J., K. & L. Which of these writers makes the most helpful contribution to the discussion?

Police and Juries

A. Which points made by Lord Parker are specifically criticisms of the jury system, and which points are irrelevant to this issue?

If the suspended sentence system, like the one described here, were adopted, would juries be less likely to convict?

What is the point of Lord Parker's comment about an outcry if a judge acquitted a policeman?

B. & C. On what main points do these writers agree? Would it be reasonable to argue that giving the police greater powers might *not* result in less 'fixing' of evidence?

E. Would it be a fair summary of Mr. Eddy's views to say: Juries work under severe handicaps, but it is better to acquit guilty men rather than to give the police extra powers?

F. Is Mr. Oerton disagreeing with any point made by Mr. Kennedy?

Is he suggesting that juries acquit guilty people because the penal system is faulty? Or is he starting on a new subject altogether?

G., H. & I. Have Freud, commando training, and 'large corporations' anything to do with the original topic? What subject is now being discussed?

General

Consider the professions and political views of the writers in relation to the views they express here.

Which four or five of these writers would make an interesting panel to discuss the problem further? Imagine what sort of course the discussion would take. What questions would you like to put to them to explore their views further?

Compare this collection of letters with a collection from *The Guardian*. Is there any clear difference of tone, or attitude? Do you feel that there is a difference of political or social background of the writers concerned?

Do recent changes in the law concerning juries affect the arguments in any way?

Problems of the Aged

B. Mrs. Bull recommends 'integration'. Why does ordinary society not always provide the kind of integration she means?

C. Does Lord Gage succeed in justifying 'purpose-built bungalows'? Does the 'gratitude' of the tenants, in itself, justify them?

D. Could schemes like the one in operation at Arthur Bliss House solve many of the problems of the aged on a *national* scale?